RHODES

THE ISLAND OF
THE SUN

MYTHOLOGY - ARCHAEOLOGY -
HISTORY
and
TOURIST GUIDE

ATHENS

ISBN 960—7310—92—6

BY CHR. Z. MATHIOULAKIS

COPYRIGHT: I. MATHIOULAKIS & Co
ADRESSE: ANDROMEDAS 1 VYRONAS 162 31
                 TEL. 7661351 - 7227229
                 ATHENS - GRECE
TRADUCTION: GEORGOS ANDONIADIS

RHODES

THE ISLAND OF
THE SUN

INDEX

RHODES

At the southeastern edge of the Aegean Sea, at a distance of less than twenty kilometers from the shores of Asia Minor lies the island of the sun and the sea. The jewel of Greek tourism and the idylic island of the Mediterranean, Rhodes has become the world's beloved island.

Drenched in the sunlight of its patron god, the god of the sun, and garbed in glittering emerald green, the island rises from the misty foam of the lapping waves. The native land of Kleovoulou and Doriea at the time when it was known by the names of Ethrea, Atavyria, Oloessa, Ophioussa (derived from the fact that the island once had so many snakes), Piessa, Pelagiou, Stadia and Telehina in antiquity. Even the island's present name is not contemporary but yet another ancient name which had been given to her.

Legend and tradition, myth and history, truth and entrancing fairy tales all merge together and become one with the existance of this magical island which has lovers from the four corners of the world.

The entire island is a marvel of sites. Each civilization which has flourished in the Mediterranean as early as the Bronze Age has left its indelible mark upon Apollo's island.

The ancient and medieval monuments also add to the island's splendour and mystique. The lost monument of the Colossal statue of the Sun god at one time gave the inhabitants' their name for Paul the Apostle in his letters addresses the christian inhabitants of the island as "Colossians".

The island's long summers, temperate climate, diversity of its landscape, breathtaking beaches, efficiently organised and managed tourist beaches and the multifarious range of entertainment found each year bring more Rhodian enthusiasts to the island.

To fully see the island, one must have several days at his disposal without the least possibility of becoming bored or tired for each step he takes brings him face to face with a different aspect of the island, presenting him with unforgetable images, images which only magicians can conjure. But then was it not on Rhodes that the most famous magicians in Greek mythology, the Telchines, chose to live?

ACCESS TO THE ISLAND

BY SHIP

Rhodes is situated approx-

imately 260 nautical miles from Pireaus. The journey by ship lasts 22 hours with several scheduled trips to and from the island each week. During the summer there are several daily departures. The island is also linked with the other islands of the Dodekanisa (twelve islands) by means of hydrofoils (flying dolphins) as well as larger liners.

The island is also linked with the Cycladic islands of Mykonos, Paros and Santorini, as well as the islands of the western Aegean such as Lesbos, Chio, Samo and Crete and with Macedonian Kavala which is situated in the northern mainland.

Lastly, access to Turky, Cyprus and Israel is also possible from Rhodes.

BY AIR

Several daily flights depart for Rhodes from Athens. The trip is both comfortable and quick. Flights from Thessaloniki, Crete, Mykonos, Santorini, Paros, Lesbos, Kos, Karpatho and Kaso also depart for Rhodes. Lastly Rhodes has scheduled flights from Cyprus, Israel and all the other countries of Western Europe.

The medieval windmills on the pier of St. Nicholas

SIZE — POPULATION — ADMINISTRATION

The island of **Rhodes** is long and narrow, stretching out in a northwesterly to southeasterly direction. Its total area is 1,398 square kilometers. It is the fourth largest Greek island after Crete, Eubia and Lesbos. The island's coastline is 220 kilometers long with a maximum width of 37 kilometers and the shortest length of 77 kilometers. The island's total population is approximately 70,000 inhabitants.

The seat of the island's administration is the Dodekanisa which is a province. The captial of the province is **Rhodes.** Other significant centres on the island are the towns of **Trianda, Aphantou, Archaggelos, Kremasti** and many others.

MOUNTAINS

The landscape of Rhodes is neither mountainous nor flat. Most of the landscape is made up of low fertile hills with small plateaus. The highest mountain on the island is Mount **Ataviros** (1,215m) and to the northeast the extension of Mount Ataviros named The **Prophet Ilias** (800m). The beaches on the island are very hospitable.

CAPES AND GULFS

The most significant capes on the island are those of Zonari located on the northeastern tip of the island, the shores of Asia Minor are located a mere 10 nautical miles away. The capes of Archaggelos, Sts. Amilianos and Larthos located on the eastern shores of the island; The cape of Prasonisi on the southwestern side of the island and the cape of Armenistis on the western side.

Of the harbours and ports which indent the 220 kilometer long coastline, the most significant are Kalitheas, Aphantou, Arhagelos, Malonos, Vlihon, Lindo and Larthou, all located on the eastern shoreline; Apolakias and Trianda, both located on the western shoreline.

CLIMATE

It was not coincidental that during antiquity the island was dedicated to the sun god. The amount of sunlight the island receives during any given years is not rivalled by any other island in the Aegean Sea. There is sunlight every day of the year. The climate is temperate, with mild winters and not too hot summers.

WATER

Rhodes receives the hightest rainfall in comparison to the other islands of the Aegean Sea. Despite this fact there is not a single river on the entire island. Only small streams and channels flow through the landscape. Nor are there any lakes on the island. There are however a great many wells which make up for this. There are healing springs at Kalithea, 12 kilometers from the city of Rhodes. The spring's efficient facilities are set in a truly idyllic landscape.

PRODUCTS

The island of Rhodes with its temperate and mild climate, refreshing rainfalls and fertile landscape is well developed in agriculture and husbandry. The inhabitants of the island, apart from their activities in commerce and shipping which were their main productive sources of wealth during times of prosperity, also exploited their fertile lands. The agricultural and husbandry products sufficed in amount to meet the needs of the islanders and all the surplus was exported.

As well the cultivation of the olive tree has from antiquity been yet another product which has brought wealth to the islanders.

Of all the agricultural products such as fruit, cereals etc, grape orchards are far the most abundant in quantity and superior in quality. The wines and sparkling wines of Rhodes are well reknown.

Agriculture has only one rival on the island and that is tourism. Tourism today makes up the largest single source of income for the island. Hotels, small industries which produce local traditional crafts and a variety of other crafts and services which are directly associated with tourism engages a great deal of the islands commercial and labour resources.

MYTHOLOGY

A rich mythology is associated with the island of Rhodes. If for each myth we isolate the purely mythological aspect which the narrative focuses on, then we begin to discern that no historical event occured on the island which was not reflected in its Mythology.

Today mythology is further supplemented and supported by place names and archeological artifacts which have been brought to light. Most of the placenames are pre-Greek, a great many of which have survived to the present such as the names **Ialisos, Kamiros** etc. The roots of Rhodian mythology can be traced back to the period prior to the Greeks and end with the colonisation of the island by the Greek Dorians.

The Telchines were considered to be one of the first inhabitants of the islands. These strange demonic creatures of Greek mythology reached Rhodes after they had been driven off of the island of Crete. They were considered to be spirits of the wind and metal, skilled in both metallurgy and the plastic arts. Hence they were considered to be the first craftsmen of marble who taught men how to work metal and stone. Their names, very aptly, were Chrisos (Gold), Argyros (Silver) and Halkos (Bronze).

Diodorus of Sicily writes that the Telchines had inspired many crafts and had taught many innovations which were useful to mankind. As metallurgists they had forged the sickle which Cronos used to emasculate Uranus as well as Poseidon's trident. In collaboration with the Cyclopes they made the "Harpy", the necklace which was given to Harmony on her wedding day. The Telchines the metallurgists were far more useful to men than the Telchines the magicians for as magicians they were hideously foul and repellent in form who made philtres out of roots, caused rain, hail and snow to fall as well as thunderbolts. They also had the gift of assuming, at will, whatever form they wanted. A malicious glance was enough to bring about terrible disasters. Amphibious creatures, they lived on the earth as well as in the water without any difficulty.

These beasts of the underworld, which taught men the art of forging metal and struck terror and fear by way of their magic, had a sister named Alia. Alia caught the eye of Poseidon the god of the sea. From their union six sons and a daughter, named Rhodes, were born. The sun god fell in love with Poseidon's daughter and gave new life to the island which had been destroyed by the Telchines.

From the union of **Rhodes** and the Sun God the Iliades were born who succeeded the Telchines. The Iliades distinguished themselves as brave sailors and shrewd merchants.

How the Illiades came to inhabit the island is narrated by **Pindar** in another myth.

When Zeus divided the world among the other gods, the god Helios was not present. The consequence of his absence was that Zeus forgot him completely. That night when Helios returned to Mount Olympus exhausted the injustice done to him was realis-

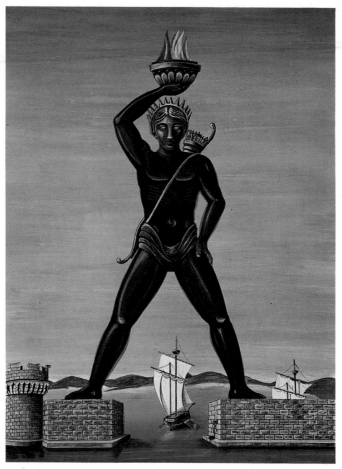

A reproduction of the Colossus, the work of the Lindian sculptor Chare.
Its height was 31 meters and it was destroyed in 226 BC

ed. Zeus, wanting to make amends, decided that he would cast lots again, but Helios did not let him. He only asked Zeus to promise him that the land which was to rise out of the sea's depths would be his. Zeus did not refuse him this request and granted him the island. This island was Rhodes, named after the nymph Rhodes, the daughter of Amphitrite and Poseidon and who was the lover of Helios. The children born to Rhodes and Helios were the Iliades, the first inhabitants of Rhodes. One of the Iliades, Kerkaphos, had three sons: Lindos, Ialisos and Kamiro. Each one built a city which bore his name. Lindos built Lindos, Ialysos built Ialyso and Kamiros built Kamiro. In another version of the myth Pindar states that there were seven Iliades: Ohimos, Kerkaphos, Aktis, Makara, Kanthalos, Triopis and Tenagis. Yet another version of the same myth claims that Kanthalou was in fact named Phaethon.

The Phoenicians were also early inhabitants of the island during the pre-Greek period. The passage of this sea faring people of the eastern Mediterranean through Rhodes is also reflected in the myths of their king Cadmus.

As Cadmus was travelling on the sea his ship was caught in a terrible storm. The king prayed to Poseidon, the god of the sea, to save him and his companions from the rage of the waves, promising that wherever he landed safely, there would he erect a temple of great magnificence in the god's honour. The god heard his prayers and guided him safely to an island. This island was Rhodes. Cadmus and his companions fulfilled their vow and built the temple. They did not confine themselves only to the building of the temple of Poseidon and so the sea faring Phonicians also built other temples in honour of the sacred Athena. The temple at Lindos was dedicated to her as well as a number of votive offerings among which was a bronze basin, an ancient crafted piece which had an inscription along the side in Phonician script. Diodorus describes this basin althoug he does not describe how it was made. According to legend the inscription on this basin was the means by which pheonician script was first introduced to the Greek area.

Although Cadmus departed from the island he left many of his companions behind to look after the temple of Poseidon.

A narrow street in the Old City

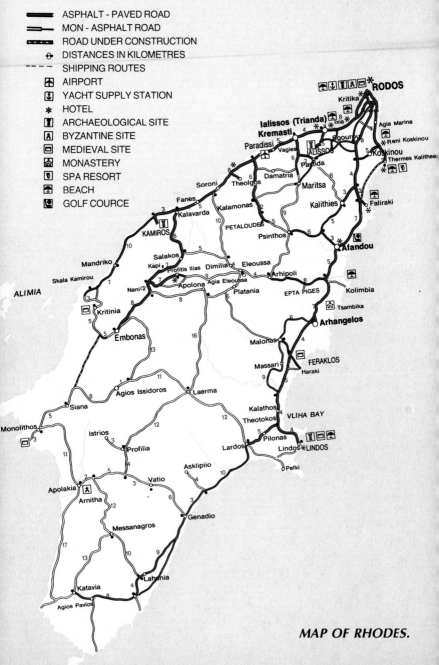

KEY TO MAP

	ASPHALT - PAVED ROAD
	MON - ASPHALT ROAD
	ROAD UNDER CONSTRUCTION
	DISTANCES IN KILOMETRES
	SHIPPING ROUTES
	AIRPORT
	YACHT SUPPLY STATION
	HOTEL
	ARCHAEOLOGICAL SITE
	BYZANTINE SITE
	MEDIEVAL SITE
	MONASTERY
	SPA RESORT
	BEACH
	GOLF COURCE

MAP OF RHODES.

KEY TO MAP OF TOWN OF RODOS

1. N.T.O.G. and Tourist Police
2. Post Office
3. Telecommunications (O.T.E.)
4. OLYMPIC AIRWAYS offices
5. Governor's palace
6. Town Hall
7. Bishop's Residence
8. Church of the Evangelismos
9. New Market Piace
10. National Theatre
11. Folk Dances Theatre
12. Sound and Light
13. Aquarium
14. Archaeological Museum
15. Byzantine Museum
16. Popular Decorative Art Collection
17. Library
18. Palace of the Grand Masters
19. Temple of Venus
20. Inn of the Knights of Auvergne
21. Byzantine Church
22. Temple of Apollo
23. Ancient Stadium
24. Ancient Theatre
25. Castellania and fountain
26. Suleiman's Mosque
27. Mourad Reis Mosque
28. The site of the Colossus of Rodos
29. Agios Nikolaos Lighthouse
30. Yacht Club

One of the many names Rhodes was known by was also Ophioussa a name derived from the great number of snakes on the island. According to myth these snakes were destroyed by the deer which the Thracian colonists brought with them when they came to the island. From that moment onwards the figure of the deer was and still is a popular decorative symbol used by the Rhodians.

ARCHITECTURE

Although Rhodes is an island of the Aegean, it has developed its own unique style of architecture which has nothing in common with the typical Aegean architecture whose characteristic feature is its picturesqueness.

A crossroad for people and civilizations, the island was ruled either by its native inhabitants or by people from other countries whose cultural and social influences were absorbed by the island during the course of its long history. This is one of the main reasons why the island's architecture has followed its own development. This unique development has given its own beauty to Rhodian buildings both public and private.

The climate, the landscape, the needs of the inhabitants and the foreign social and cultural influences all lent to the creation of a particular type of house compatible with Rhodian society. At times the type varies from region to region depending on the needs of the inhabitants. Thus it is not unusual to see neighbouring houses which have small or great differences not only in terms of basic construction but also in terms of design.

Throughout the island's different historical periods the popular architectual tradition reflects the social structure and aesthetic tastes of the people. In many mountainous villages the houses are indicative of the social background and popular aesthetic tastes of an age which is quickly disappearing. A house with a high wall surrounding it is indicative of a closed society whereas a house with a low wall or no wall surrounding it at all is reflective of an open society, a society which recieves external influences and attitudes much easier than the former.

All building materials used by the craftsmen in times passed and indeed still used by the present craftsmen come from the surrounding landscape. Stone, soil and wood are skillfully used to construct a house which is compatible with the island's climate, the needs of the inhabi-

The Road of the Knights

tants and the aesthetic tastes while simultaneously respecting the natural environment from which these building materials were taken from.

The simple elongated rectangular structure whose entrance and main facade is on one of the longer sides of the rectangal is one of the most popular types.

HISTORY

The first inhabitants on the island appeared during the Paleolithic period. Very few Neolothic settlements and remains have been discovered on the island and these which have been discovered, were discovered by chance. But if very little has been documented from the Neolithic period the Pre-historic Period has a rich source of remains which have helped to piece together quite accurately a vivid picture of the pre-historic and pre-Greek period. Almost all the people of the Eastern Mediterranean, Carians, Pheonicians, Lydians and Minoans from Crete, have at one time left traces of their stay on Rhodes. All these races not only used the island as a stepping stone but also created their own civilizations with individual developments either as sailors, merchants, clay artists, metallurgists etc. or as cultivators of the earth and olives. They had ties with practically all of the eastern

Mediterranean.

The first Greek inhabitants on the island arrived in the 15th century BC and were Myceneans from the Argolid. These people were the Greek Acheans who had conquored and absorbed all the pre Greek races on the mainland and the islands of Greece. The Acheans built the acropolis of Ialysos, and named it Achaia, a name which did not change even after the Dorians came onto the island. The Acheans developed a flourishing civilization and distinguished themselves as sailors and merchants. They had ties and commercial dealings with the people along the coast of Asia Minor and the Pheonicians and even with the Pharaohs of Egypt as two scarabs (pieces of jewelry) bear out which were found, one at Kamiro and the other at Ialysos.

The descent of the Dorians, the second largest Greek speaking tribe, threw Greece into confusion around 1,100 BC. The exact arrival of the Dorians onto the island of Rhodes is not known but it is estimated that they arrived soon after they established themselves in the Peloponnese. The Dorians, using the plains of Argolid in the Peloponnese and more particularly Tiryns as their base, drove many of the Acheans the islands of the Aegean from Sea and from areas on the island of Crete. On Rhodes they established their supremacy and drove out or lessened the number of Acheans present on the island. The possession of Rhodes by the Dorians is marked by the building of Ialysos, Kamiro and Lindos, the three most significant cities which became the administrative and cultural centres of the island. Lindos, apart from being a commerical and cultural centre, was also the main religous centre for the worship of the goddess Athena. The famous temple of **Lindian Athena** was located here.

In 700 BC the cities in Asia Minor established the Ionian Alliance, or more commonly known as the "Pan Ionian Alliance" whose centre was the sacred temple of Poseidon Elikoniou in Mykali. This alliance forced the Dorians of Lindos, Ialysos, Kamiro, Kos and Halicarnassus to establish their own alliance, the so called Dorian Hexapolis-a federation of cities which had a political and religious character and whose administrative centre was the sanctuary of Apollo Triopios near the peninsula of Knidos. The establishment of this alliance, if anything else, demonstrates that

A view of the New City

Agiou Phanouriou Street

the two Greek tribes of the Dorians and Ionians did not occupy the same area in peaceful harmony. As well it should be noted that during this period the Greek tribes did not have to defend their territories or interest against other races as they had in the past.

The political stability and economic development of the cities on Rhodes, particularly Lindos, allowed the ambitious and restless Dorians to seek out other areas for wealth and power outside the boundaries of the island. In 691-690 BC Lindos sent its first colonists to the western Mediterranean thus establishing the cities of Gela in Sicily and Phasele on the shores of Pamphilia in Asia Minor. The rulers of the colonies were two brothers, Antirimos who ruled over the colonies of Sicily and Lakios who ruled over the colonies established at Phasele. For many centuries these two colonies maintained close ties with the mother country.

The city of **Lindos** greatly flourished during the time of **Kleoboulos** who is considered to be one of the seven Sages of ancient Greece. (The other six were Vias the Priineus, Thalis the Milissios, Periandros the Corinthian, Pittakos the Mytiliano,

The screen of Pythian Apollo

Solon the Athenian and Herlon the Lacadamonian.) Kleboulos was born in 600 BC and died in 530 BC. He wrote approximately 3000 riddles and epigrams. The son of Euagora, he believed himself to be a true Dorian and claimed direct decent from Hercules. For fourty years he was the tyrant ruler of Lindos. As a "tyrant" he gained great fame throughout Greece as a wise and moderate politician. Deeply pious, as his fellow countrymen, he rebuilt the temple of Athena and dedicated to her as votive offerings the spoils of his campaign in Asia Minor against Lykias. There was a poem which was called the "Chelidonisma", a poem set to music which the young children of ancient Rhodes used to sing to welcome the swallows in the spring and which was attributed to Kleoboulos. The tyranny of Kleoboulos was not a tyranny by the contemporary meaning of the word, nor should it be considered as such. Honoured by his fellow countrymen during his life and after his death, he is considered to be one of the greatest men of the ancient world.

The threat to the total supremacy which the Greek races had over the islands of the eastern Aegean and along the coast of

The aquarium.

Orpheos Street the ideal street for a stroll

Asia Minor appeared in the 6th century BC. This threat came not from an indigenous people but from an invading race. It was during this period that the Persians first appeared in the area. Cares, Lydians, Phrygians and yet other tribes from Asia Minor with whom the Dorians and Ionians did not live in harmony. Dorians and Ionians fell under their subjugation and entire cities lost their independance. Rhodes also received the invading people and in 491 BC the Persians, led by Dati, beseiged the island. The courageous resistence of the Rhodians and the miraculous in-tervention of the goddess Athena saved not only Lindos but the entire island from falling under the Persian yoke. According to the chronicles of Rhodes the beseiged Rhodians exhausted their fresh water supplies and the threat of thirst to the enclosed people loomed before them. The sortage of drinking water was a well known fact to the encamped Persians who patiently waited for the city to surrender. It was then that the goddess' miraculous in-tervention delivered the city. Athena appeared in a dream to a nobleman of Lindos and told him that if the city held out a little longer she would help them by begging her father Zeus to send the water that the city had such great need of. The Lindians took stock of their remainig water supplies and sent word to the Persian leader that the city would surrender to him within five days if Athena did not send the water she had promised them. To Dati this seemed nonsense but nontheless agreed to the Lindian appeal. The next day thick dark clouds covered the sky over Lindos and not long after a tremendous rainstorm broke out. The rain fall in torrents, but only above the Acropolis of the city.

This was the indisputable sign that Athena's aid to the city had arrived. In the face of this divine manifestation the Persian army had no choice but to end the seige and to agree to terms of friendship with the Lindians for "these people are surely protected by the gods". Rich votive offerings were piously offered to the goddess' temple by the Persians in the hope that she would forgive their impiety.

During the Persian Wars the position adopted by Rhodes was not the same as that adopted by them during the Persian siege led by Dati. Not only did they not al-

A view of the Old City

ly themselves with their fellow Greeks, they actively supported the Persians in their attack on Greece. Perhaps they felt that Athena would not help them as she had in the past. Thus the Rhodian fleet which was made up of 40 ships took part in the Battle of Salamina in 480 BC but as an ally of the Persian king Xerxes. Two years later the Rhodians, albeit Dorians, became members of the Athenian Alliance of 478 BC. For several years the three Rhodian cities remained loyal to Athens. During the Peloponnesian War, the longest civil war which divided the Greeks and which began in 431 and lasted until 407, Rhodes changed allegiance and entered into a Spartan Alliance. One of the most significant events, indeed if not the most significant, occured in 408 BC. The people of Lindos, Ialysos and Kamiro finally realised an old dream they had cherished: the founding of a new city. This event passed into the island's history by the name of "Sinikismos" and constituted a landmark in the history of the island. One of the central figures whose personal initiative and impetus was pivotal to the founding of this new city was a reknown Rhodian citizen named Dorieus.

DORIEUS

This illustrious Rhodian was a

descendant of the Eratides, a reknown family throughout Greece because of their many victories in the Olympic Games. Founder of this family of Olympic victors was **Diagoras** who was much praised by Pindar. Diagoras and his son Dorieus were "Periodonikes" that is they had both won in all four Olympic Games (Olympus, Isthmia, Py-

The large beach at Rhodes

thia and Nemea). Dorieus' two brothers, Damagitos and Akousilaos, were also Olympic victors. Indeed it is said that during the Olympic Games in 448 BC Damagitos and Akousilaos were both declared victors on the same day, the former in pangratio (a combination of boxing and wrestling) and the latter in boxing. Both men lifted theïr father on their shoulders and walked around the stadium while the spectators showered them with flowers. One spectator from Lacedomia cried out, "Die Diagora lest you should want to ascend to Olympus!". Not only were the father and sons victors

Mosaic depicting the mask of a Satyr
Roman mosaic from Kos depicting the Muse Thalea

in the Olympic games but Diagora's nephews also recieved the Olympic laurel crown. The statues of all six Olympic victors stood at Olympia until the 2nd century AD.

Diagoras saw to it that a longer more lasting monument was erected in his and his family's honour. When in 464 BC he won the boxing match in the Olympic Games, he asked Pindar to compose the hymn in honour of his victory. This hymn by Pindar was one of the greatest honours ever given not only to the victor but to his country as well. Such a moving hymn composed by such an illustrious poet made not only Diagoras and his family proud but all Rhodians. This hymn was engraved in gold letters on a marble stele which stood in the temple of Athena at Lindos.

Dorieus, who had been declared the victor of three consecutive Olympic Games (432, 428 and 424 BC, winner eight times at Isthmia, seven times at Nemea and "unchallenged" in Pythia, "unchallenged" because no competitor stepped forth to challenge him and so he was declared the victor) took part in the Peloponnesian War as an ally of Sparta. The Athenians who had not been driven off the island of Rhodes condemned him to death in 425 BC. In order to save his life he fled the island

and took refuge with the Throusious of Lower Italy. In 414 BC after the destruction of the Athenians in Sicily, he sailed along with ten triremes to Simi where he met up with the Spartan fleet. In the naval battle which followed the Spartan fleet emerged victorious. After this Spartan victory, Dorieus returned to his native island of Rhodes where he successfully pursuaded his fellow countrymen to enter into the Spartan Alliance and played a decisive part in the unification of the three major cities of Rhodes and the founding of the new city. In 407 the Athenians successfuly captured Dorieus and held him prisoner. Although he had been condemned to death in 425 BC they granted the Olypic victor his life. Later on the oligarchical Dorieus abandoned the Spartans and his oligarchical family and actively supported the Athenian Alliance. In 396 BC he once again excercised political influence on his fellow Rhodians and pursuaded them to foresake Sparta and become allies of Athens. The Spartans, in retaliation, captured the now aging Dorieus and held him prisoner. Oligarchical Sparta did not hold the glorious Dorieus in high estime and so they condemned and put to death this illustrious old man who was so respected throughout Greece.

The death of Dorieus however did not alter Rhode's position and a little later she became an ally of Athens and a member of the Second Athenian Alliance.

RHODES

The new city was built on the south eastern akrotiri of the island and stands on the site of the ancient city. The city was named Rhodes and was built according to the plans of the architect Hippodamou of Milito. In no time the city developed into a large financial, commercial and cultural centre in the eastern Mediterranean. The history of the island from this point onwards is closely linked with the history of this city. This new public administrative centre, was named "The Municipality of Rhodes". The three older cities which had jointly founded this new one still maintained their own municipalities but they had only one church which was the church of the Municipality of Rhodes which elected the administrative leaders and the five prytanies, all of whom served in office for six months. Only the eponymous lord, who was also a high priest to Helios the sun god, served a one year term of office. There was a local body of government which was elected into office by the former inhabitants of the founding cities. These officials were called "Mastrous" and they were the ones who dealt with the individual internal issues of the city.

In the fourth century BC a great political upheaval was marked on the island of Rhodes. The consequence of this upheaval was the constant change of the alliances established by Rhodes. Thus from 396 until 391 BC Rhodes was an ally of Democratic Athens while from 391 to to 378 BC the island was an ally of oligarchic Sparta. In 378 BC

Roman statue of the Goddess Hygeia

Rhodes once again entered into an alliance with Athens, an alliance which lasted until 357 BC. In 357 BC Masolos, the Satrap of Karia, tried to incorporate Rhodes into his territories. Although Masolos was unsuccessful, his wife and heir, Artemisia, was not. She defeated the Rhodian fleet and seized the city. Soon after her victory she put to death all pominent Rhodians and set up trophies of victory in the centre of the city.

Until 340 Rhodes was part of the Satrapy of Karia. From the middle of the 4th century AD and onwards the history of Greece was dominated by the appearance of Philip II's Macedonians and the descendants and heirs of Alexander the Great. The Rhodian brothers Mentor and Memnon offered their services as mercenaries to the Persian King against Alexander's campaign into Greece. The official Rhodian policy at the beginning of the war was one of neutrality. This neutral position was adopted primarily because of the city's commercial interests. Alexander's decisive victories brought the Rhodians to the side of the Greeks and King Alexander received the Rhodians in friend-

The Old Harbour

ship, adding their fleet to the Greek navy. Upon the death of Alexander the Great a new chapter of flourishing wealth and power is added to the island's history.

THE HELLENISTIC AND ROMAN YEARS

The period which followed was a period of wealth and development for Rhodes. The political policies the island adopted was dictated by her commercial interests. The Rhodians tried to maintain a neutral position throughout the various clashes and upheavals which occured in the eastern Mediterranean at this time. The desire to maintain neutrality and to protect their commerical interests and activities are the two characteristic features of Rhodian "foreign policy". This neutral stance was not always advantageous to the island particularly during the civil wars between the various Roman generals. Rhodes was often the victim of these internal Roman struggles. The Roman civil clashes however were not the main sources of destruction on the island. She was also plagued by the various enemies of Rome.

Upon the death of Alexander the Great Rhodes was caught in the middle of the civil war which broke out among the heirs of the Macedonian king and which resulted in the siege of the city by Demetrius in 305 BC.

General view of the harbour.

The Palace of the Grand Masters

34

The marble head of the sun god Helios.
Archaeological Museum of Rhodes

Aphrodite of Rhodes, 1st century BC.
Museum of Rhodes

THE SIEGE OF RHODES BY DEMETRIUS

The Siege of Rhodes by Demetrius the Besieger, the son of Antigonus the one eyed, marked one of the most significant victories in the island's military history.

The siege carried out by the Antigonians lasted one year, from 305 to 304 BC and ended in a compromise between the city and the Antigonians. The reason for this attack on the city was Rhodes' refusal to enter into a military alliance with Antigonus the King of Syria against Ptolemy Sotiros I, King of Egypt. This dramatic siege is chronicled in great detail by Diodorus. For a whole year Demetrius lauched army and naval attacks against the city in an attempt to capture Rhodes. During the course of the siege Demetrius, a brilliant general who was reknown for his military force and genius, failed to capture the city and crush the heroic defense of the beseiged Rhodians despite the use of the most modern, for that period, siege machinery. The Rhodians, aided by Antigonus' rival, Ptolemy, and several other Greek city states, forced Demetrius to accept as mediators several Greek city states and to reach a compromise between himself and the besieged city. In this compromise between Demetrius and Rhodes, both Ptolemy and Antigonus played decisive roles as councillors.

The intervention of the Greek city states and the peace proposals set forth by both Antigonus and Ptolemy enabled the two sides to reach a settlement without either of the two loosing face.

Demetrius departed from the island leaving behind his famous siege machines. These were sold by the Rhodians and from the proceeds the islanders built an immense bronze statue of the god Helios. This statue, the famous **Colossus of Rhodes**, was the work of Chares of Lindos, the pupil of Lysippos.

The island's wealth, naval strength and cultural prosperity made Rhodes one the most powerful centres in the area. A great part of commercial trade passed through into the island's hands and its currency became one of the strongest and most stable. The Rhodian Code of Maritime Law became accepted as the International Maritime Law in the Mediterranean. Acts drawn from the code were later adopted by the Romans and Byzantine Emperors.

The year 227 BC was a year of disaster for the city of Rhodes. An earthquake leveled the beautiful city to the ground. This earth-

Rhodian wine vessel, 7th century BC

Rhodian plate

Rhodian pot of the Phikellouras type, 6th century BC

quake was so violent that there was a possiblity that the city would never recover by its own resources. This disaster moved the people and rulers of the entire area who all felt that it was their bounded duty to aid the Rhodians in rebuilding their city, more grand and beautiful than before its destruction by the earthquake. Thus a new city was built in no time with the determination of the inhabitants and the generous aid given to them from abroad. Only the Colossus remained where it had fallen as a reminder of the disaster. For 800 years the statue remained thus, primarily due to an oracle which forbade the inhabitants from setting it up again. In 653 AD Arab pirates broke up the remains of Chares of Lindos' statue and sold it as scrape metal. This was the end of the glorious statue of the god Helios. A work of art, it is now considered to be one of the seven wonders of the ancient world. At about the time of the statue's destruction, another great power emerged in Greece. This power was Rome. Faithful to the policies which ensured the island's commercial interest, Rhodes had no choice but to establish friendly relations with the Romans. This new power obliged the island to view Rome's enemies as Rhode's enemies. The Rhodians fought against Philip V of Macedonia and later Antiochus III of Syria as reluctant allies of Rome. Indeed the navy of Rhodes, led by Eudamo, played a decisive role in the naval battle in 190 BC which took place at Sidi in Asia Minor and which destroyed Antiochus' fleet. The man who faced Eudamo was one of the greatest enemies of Rome, Hannibal. The story of how Hannibal came to be at the court of Antiochus is well known. The years which followed were prosperous ones for the island, but her prosperity depended primarily on the good will of Rome. Primarily due to Rome's benevolent consent, Rhodes was a supreme power in the area of the Aegean Sea and in some areas of Asia Minor. But Rome's goodwill did not last for very long. After the battle of Pydnas in 168 BC where the Roman General Aemilias Paulos crushed Perseus, the Romans punished their reluctant "ally". Lykia and Caria were removed from Rhodian jurisdiction and the port of Delos was declared a free port in 166 BC. This was a fatal blow to Rhodian commerce since the harbour taxes which were collected by Rhodes seized to exist. The loss of this income heralded the

The Old City: Socratou Street and the Suleiman Mosque

economic decline of the city. Never again was Rhodes to regain her economic strength. Forced to bend to Roman will, Rhodes was compelled to sign a treaty obliging the island to have the same friends and foes as Rome. What this treaty did was to effectively eliminate the political freedom of the island. Striped of her power to decree her own fate, Rhodes fought alongside the Romans in the third Punic War against Carthage and the campaigns against the king of Pontus, Mithridates, whose pirate allies relentlessly raided the island while Mithridates himself laid an unsuccesful siege to it. Pompey's victory in 63 BC put an end to the raids on Rhodes by fierce pirates.

The treaty of 166 BC effectively solved the problem of who was Rhodes' friend and who was her enemy, but it did not solve the problem of Rhodes' delicate relationship with Rome herself when Roman Imperial generals turned against each other. Roman civil strife usually brought destruction to Rhodes.

In the clash between Caesar and Pompey the Rhodians favoured Pompey. Upon Caesar's victory over Pompey in 48 BC at Pharsalus Caesar did not punish the Rhodians but renewed the treaty with them and allowed the island the same liberties that the

treaty of 166 BC had granted them. The same did not occur however with Cassius. When the island refused Cassius the aid he and Brutus sought against the allies of the murdered Caesar, Cassius in rage destroyed the Rhodian fleet and attacked and conquered the city. What followed was wreakage and plunder on an unprecedented scale. Thousands of Rhodians lost their lives and valuable art treasures were plundered and carried off to Italy. According to tradition, the enraged Cassius left only the statue of the sun god Helios to the city. The god Helios did not forgive this Roman's destruction of his city and in 42 BC at Philipii Octavian and Anthony defeated the ravagers of Rhodes. Their defeat forced them to commit suicide. Upon hearing of their deaths, the Rhodians joyfully celebrated the victory of Octavian and Anthony in the sacred temples, believing that their island had finally attained peace. In this they were mistaken and once again the Romans set upon each other. When Octavian defeated Anthony and Cleopatra at Actium in 31 BC he granted the island its local autonomy, although the island had not allied itself with him in the struggle.

This secured autonomy was held by the Rhodians until 297 AD whereupon Diocletian delegated the island to the Empire's Island Province.

Augustus proclaimed the island as a place of exile for prominent Roman citizens. Such distinguished citizens as Tiberius (before he was proclaimed Emporer), Cicero and many others spent several years as exiles on the island of Rhodes. The earthquake of 155 AD brought to an end the island's long and bright period in history. The raid by pirates in 263 BC and the loss of her autonomy did not have adverse effects upon the island nor did it bring about its decline, for the island's decline had begun much earlier and nothing could have worsened it or checked it.

MEDIEVAL AND LATER YEARS

During the Middle Ages Rhodes fell into total obscurity. The island did not play a decisive role in the affairs of the Eastern Mediterranean as it had in the past. It nonetheless remained an independent island within the vastness of the Byzantine State. The capital of a Province during

The funerary Stele of Timarista and her daughter Krito (5th century BC) from the Cemetery of Kamiro.

the time of Diocletian, it remained the captial during the period of the Byzantine Empire. Information about the island during this period can be gleaned from historical sources written by several Imperial chroniclers. They were however more interested in recording what happened in the state capital and less interested in what was happening in the provinces. Local events were referred to only when they directly influenced the events in the capital. This does not mean that the provinces did not take an individual active part in the life of the state.

In 515 AD Rhodes once again was struck by an earthquake which completely destroyed the city. Emporer Anastasios came to the aid of the devasted city and with public funds from the imperial State all public buildings in the city were rebuilt. This Imperial support however did not prove sufficient to revive the life of the city. Despite the devastation, several years later the potters of the city sent clay tiles needed for the roof of the church of Agia Sophia in Constantinople.

Persians led by Chosroes first arrived to the island at the beginning of the 7th century AD. The victory of the Byzantine Emperor Heracliou put an end to hostilities towards the island. Not soon afterwards new invaders appeared, this time in the guise of the Arab Moabiah. Leading the faithful of Mohammad, Moabiah arrived to Rhodes. It was Moabiah's Arabs who broke up the Colossus and sold the peices. According to legend the merchant who bought the statue's bronze pieces needed 900 camels to carry them away. Muslim pirates, the Saracens, first arrived to the island in 717-718 AD. In 718 AD the Byzantine fleet attacked and destroyed the raiders' fleet.

In 807 AD the island was sacked and seized for a short period by the Caliph Haroun al Rashid. With a large number of prisoners and invaluable spoils the Arab invader left the island.

After the invasion of 807 AD Rhodes entered into a brief period of peace and tranquility. Within the Byzantine State Rhodes developed certain commercial and naval activities. Once again the island established contact with the West. The naval powers of Venice, Genoa and Pisa maintained direct commercial contact with Rhodes. These contacts that the island established with the naval powers of the West were strengthened during the Crusades. Indeed the island sent men and ships to help the Crusaders' endevours.

Richard the Lionheart, the King

of England, and Philip. The King of France arrived with a fleet to reorganise their troops and enlist mercenaries in 1191.

In 1204 after Constantinople was conquered by the Crusaders, Rhodes was governed by Leon Gabalas. A keen and shrewd politician, Gabalas distanced himself from Theodore Laskari, the Byzantine Emperor, who had fled to Nikea in Asia Minor and declared himself Despot of the island. By proclaiming the island's independance, Gabalas in effect saved Rhodes from Venetian occupation. Gabalas remained Despot of the island until 1224. In the same year The Emperor of Nikea, Vatazis, annexed the island and incorporated it into his state, but recognising Gabalas and his heirs as Despots of the island. For approximately two decades the same status quo was maintained on the island which was established in 1224. In 1246 The Gabalians attempted to declare the island's independance and sought the aid of the Venetians. This resulted in a long period of strife between the Venetians and the Byzantines. Finally in 1261 the Byzantines recaptured Constantinople and Rhodes once

Roman mosaic from Kos depicting a hunt

Roman mosaic from Kos

again passed under the jurisdiction of the reunited Byzantine Empire. This change of administration was only figurative. In effect the real administrators were not the Imperial representatives but in fact Genoese admirals engaged by the Emperor. In 1306 the Genoese Admiral Vignoli hired by the declining Byzantine Empire sold Rhodes, Kos and Leros to the Knights of St. John of Jerusalem.

The Order of St. John of Jerusalem was first founded in Palestine sometime in the 11th century. The brotherhood's original purpose was to protect the pilgrims who travelled to the Holy Lands and their main seat was the church of St. John in Jerusalem.

During the crusades the Order developed into a military organization. With the defeat of the crusaders the Order was driven out of Palestine. The Knights expelled by the Caliph arabs first took refuge on Cyprus. From there they planned their establishment on Rhodes. In 1309 the Knights arrived to the island despite the resistence of the Greek population.

The Order consisted of three classes: The Knights (the military figures), the chaplain (ecclesiastics) and the brothers. The members of the Order were drawn

Roman mosaic from Kos

from all the Catholic countries of western Europe and were divided into national groups which were called Tongues. The offical languages of the Order were Latin and French and the Orders spiritual leader was the Pope of Rome. During the period of the Knights' rule on the island which lasted for approximately 200 years, the Order developed extensive commercial activities and Rhodes once again experienced a period of economic prosperity.

Ties were established with Western Europe and the influence the Order exerted on the island was great. Western architecture passed through to the island in its purest form and exerted a decisive influence on local architecture. The administration lay in the hands of the Grand Master who was elected for life and who was aided by a councillor whose function was that of an advisor with no real power. The peace that the Order brought with it and the prosperity to the people of this strategic island did not last for long and in 1480 the bells of war were rung below the castle of Rhodes. The invader this time was the Turkish sultan Mohammed II, the sacker of Constantinople. The Knights and the people put up a heroic resistance and the force of the attackers siege lessened below the walls of Rhodes. The Turkish Sultan withdrew in defeat. For 40 years the island retained its independance. In 1522 the Turkish Sultan Suleiman the Magnificent led a large fleet and army which set siege to the beautiful city from sea and land. The siege lasted for 6 months during which time the castle of Rhodes held out. What the Sultan did not accomplish by feats of deed he accomplished by trechery. A disgrumpled knight led the Turks to the castle's vulnerable spot. After this betrayal the battle was decided. The Knights negotiated an honouable treaty and they departed from the city together with approximately 4000 Rhodians. On December 22 the island fell under Turkish jurisdiction.

The Turkish occupation of the island was a period of decline and persecution of the christian population. It came to an end on May 4, 1912 with the arrival of the Italian army on the island. During the period of Italian occupation an attempt was made to develop the island's economy through public works such as the harbour, new roads, the establishment of hotel facilities, restoration of areas etc. The new city was developed during this time and the period of the island's exploitation as a tourist centre began. Italian rule ended in 1947 when Rhodes and the other Dodecanese were incorporated into the Greek State.

The Church of the Annunciation

The entrance to the harbour at Rhodes and the Castle of St. Nicholas

48

IALYSOS

Set in a lush fertile area over-flowing with orchards and gardens, approximately 10 klms from Mount Filerimos stood the ancient city of Ialysos.

The ancient settlement which was inhabited since prehistoric times and later became one of the three major city states on the island nestled on the south-western slope of the mountain.

High up on the mountain's flat leveled peak the acropolis of this proud ancient city was built in the 15th century BC. The only thing which remained as a reminder to these ancient people was the name of the mountain peak which survived until the Roman period. Today the Rhodians refer to the peak as the "fortress" after the castle which was built by the Byzantines and further extended and fortified by the Knights in the 14th century. The harbour of this reknown city was named Shedia. Today large hotel compounds stand along the coast.

Ialysos was an affluent city until 408 BC when the new city was established and reduced this former rich settlement to a small insignificant centre. The city of Rhodes was built in the area of Ialysos and the former city gave to the new one not only a significant number of its population but also the emblem of Rhodes. The old image which appeared on Ialysos's currency became the symbol of the new Rhodian city. The first inhabitants of the city can be traced from the realms of mythology and who most probably were the Pheonicians. The Pheonicians were succeeded by the Acheans who came from the area of the Argolid in the Peloponnessus. The settlement of the Acheans is closely associated with the myth of Iphicles and Phalanthou. When Iphicles and his ancient followers first arrived to the area he had to do battle with the Pheonicians of Phalanthou. The myth refers to this battle. The Pheonicians were haunted by an old oracle which stated that they would loose the area only after the ravens all turned white and when fish appeared in the wine jugs. The clever Iphicles took several ravens and after covering them with white plaster, set them free to fly above the city. He also bribed on of Phalanthou's servants to put fish in the wine jugs. In the face of these indisputable signs, the Pheonicians prepared to leave and Phalanthou requested from

The Gothic-style church.

The market by night.

Iphicles that he be allowed safe passages from the island. Thus the myth reflects the arrival of the Acheans to the area.

The Acheans were succeed by the Dorians, the other large Greek speaking tribe. As a Doric city, Ialysos played a decisive role in the island's historical development.

The passage of the centuries erased all visible signs of the Acheans and only the name of the acropolis remained in the minds of the Dorians as a dim memory of the first Greek tribe's stay in the area. Today archaeological excavations have unearthed remains from the Achean city in the area of the village Trianda while tombs which date from the same period have been found in the areas of Moskou Vounara and Makria Vounara. In the area of Trianda and along the canal of Daphni tombs were discovered which yielded rich artifacts. The objects unearthed allow us to confirm the fact that the civilization here was identical to that of the Mycenean civilization which flourished on the Peloponessus.

A two laned road leads up to the flattened peak of the mountain. This plateau, which has a panoramic view of the surrounding area, has been exploited as a strategic area since the time of the Pheonicians. Acheans, Dorians, Byzantine and Knights have all left indelible marks of their military exploitation of the peak. The two look out towers loom high above the southwestern corners of the triangular complex with its double Byzantine towers—remains of the once powerful Byzantine castle. It was at this Byantine castle that a violent battle took place in 1248 against the Genoese who sought to gain control of the island. This castle was used by the knights in 1306 from which they launched their attack and finally it was here that the Turkish Sultan Shuleiman the Magnificent set up his military headquarters in 1522 in his campaign to bring Rhodes under his control.

On the highest spot of the plateau the ruins of the Monastery and the church dedicated to the Virgin can be seen. This monastery was built directly above the ruins of an older Byzantine church. Near the ruins of the Knights' building one can see the ruins of yet another Byzantine Basilica. Below this church there is a small chapel which has wallpaintings which date from the 14th and 15th centuries.

Philerimos: The Monastery

These medieval structures were built on the site of a large ancient temple dated from the 3rd or 2nd century BC, built in the Doric order and dedicated to Athena Poliada and Zeus Poliea. This temple in turn was built on the ruins of yet an older temple. Of the large temple dedicated to Athena and Zeus only ruins together with the foundations and a plinth which had originally served as the base of a statue, possibly of Athena, have survived. In front of this plinth one can see the flagstones which had been laid as the floor for the older temple.

DORIC FOUNTAIN

On the eastern side of the acropolis and situated 25 to 40 meters away one can see a fountain. This fountain has been dated to the 4th century BC and is a covered fountain, the roof of which is supported by Doric columns and embellished with lion heads which served as water sprouts. On one of these columns on the interior there is an inscription which is illegible.

Local religious festivals were held in honour of the sun goddess Alectrona, a diety who most likely was introduced to the island by the Acheans from the Peloponessus. Later this festival was dedicated to Erethaniou Apollo who most likely was a pre Greek diety. In time he was associated with Apollo. Near the village of Theologo one can see the Church of God. The path to Cavalry is a stairway of 134 stone steps which are widely spaced apart. On one of its sides scenes from the Passion of Christ are depicted in relief. It is from these stone carvings that the path derived its name "Path to Cavalry".

The road which leads to the Monastery of Philerimos

KAMIROS

Another large and major city of ancient Rhodes whose founding has been lost in the depths of prehistory is Kamiros, located 37 klms from Rhodes. This old city whose period of prosperity ended when the new city was founded was first unearthed in 1860. The inhabitants of the area kept unearthing small ancient artifacts in their fields. This led to the first archaeological excavation which were begun in 1860. The excavations discovered an ancient cemetary at Fakeloura. Further excavations were conducted by Italian archaeologist which revealed a great section of this once beautiful city of mythical Althameni, the grandson of Minos and son of Katrea the king of Crete. The grandson of Minos and the son of Katrea left his native homeland after he was told of the terrible oracle which prohesised that he would kill his father. When he left Crete he came to Rhodes and landed on the island in the area of Kritinias, just south of where he built Kamiros. This area is called Leggonia today. Often when Althameni felt nostalgia for his lost homeland and native gods, he would take the path which led to the peak of Mount Attabyra. From there, on a clear day, the exiled prince of Crete could see the mountain tops of his native homeland and offer sacrifices to Zeus, the patron god of Crete, on an altar he had built on the peak of this mountain. For the inhabitants who came after him this was the temple dedicated to Atabyro Zeus. Althameni was not the only one who suffered from nostalgia. The old king of Crete, Katrea, longed to see his lost child and one day left Crete in search of him. He finally arrived in the area of Kritinias and with him the curse of the oracle. Althameni, thinking the unknown warriors to be pirates quickly killed them all. When he recognised his father among the dead he prayed to the gods to let the earth open at his feet and swallow him. The gods heard him and granted his prayer, and so the earth tore open from under him and swallowed Althameni, the founder of Kamiros. Within this legend there is a small grain of truth, for this myth documents the historical arrival of Cretans to the area. The name Kamiros is an echo of the name Ierapetra on Crete and the worship of the Milatinous gods was widespread on prehistoric Crete. Zeus Milatinos and Malia, both chthonian dieties, reveal the "underworld" characteristic which is so prevelent in all the religions of perhistoric man.

The area of Kamiros, Kamiris, was much smaller in comparison to the other two ancient cities. It was the most fertile area on the island. The worship of the Milatinous gods, the gods who taught man the reaping of wheat and the making of bread, must have had some religious associations with the agricultural production of the area. The pottery the city produced was well re-known and the commercial ties it developed with the other centres surrounding it were of great importance. Indeed the ties the city had were not limited to the island but extended as far away as Egypt and the Pharaoh. Built along the south western slopes of the mountain in an amphitheatrical manner, ancient Kamiros was an unfortified city, a city without walls. It is unknown when exactly the inhabitants abandoned this beautiful and peaceful city. To date no reason can be substantiated as to why the inhabitants left. The life of the city did not end with the foundation of the new city in 408 BC but continued well into the Roman Period.

The numerous funerary offerings which have been discovered in tombs of the area indicate that Kamiros was a rich and flourishing city from as early as the prehistoric period. From the 6th century BC onwards the city struck its own coinage upon which a fig leaf was depicted.

The excavations which were made at various times have brought to light an entire ancient city with its private and public buildings. The remains which have been discovered date from the Hellenistic and Roman Periods. Most impressive are the columns which have been replace in situ which enclose the gardens of private houses from the Hellenistic Period. Equally impressive are the city's water supply and sewage networks. Small cisterns which collected rain water and clay pipelines are all that remain of a once perfect system. In the archaeological area at a lower level, in the square of the ancient city, an altar dedicated to the sun god Helios was discovered together with a temple built in the Doric order and which dates from the 3rd century BC.

A 4th or 3rd century plinth with inscriptions as well as a stoa with surrounded columns, also with inscriptions, have been found which refer to the original founders of the city.

The remains of the large temple dedicated to Kamirados Athena, the patron goddess of the city since prehistoric time, can be discerned at the hilltop. The temple is located behind a large building which dates from

Kamiro: A view of the market and the screen

the 3rd century BC. This building is a large stoa like structure built in the Doric order with a double row of columns surrounding it. Its length on the longest side is 200m and it resembles a stoa in that in the back there are rooms and shops. Within the stoa a large cistern was found whose measurements are 38m long, 10m wide and 3m deep, and which dates from the 6th century BC. The cistern had a capacity to hold approximately 600 cubic meters of water which was more than enough to sustain 400 families during the dry months. During the Hellenistic Period the cistern was covered over. In the area just before the cistern the platform of a Hellenistic altar can be seen. It would not be an exaggeration to liken the surrounding area of Kamiros to that of the largest cemetary · of ancient Greece which has yielded many rare and valuable artifacts.

LINDOS

Lindos is located on the eastern side of the island approximately 55 klms from the city of Rhodes.·

An imposing cliff whose height is 166m rises from the level of the sea. To the left and right of this enormous crag were two harbours, one larger than the other. On the triangular surface of this giant rock the ancient Lindians worshipped their patron goddess the Lindian Athena. The temple dedicated to the goddess was impressive as it was surrounded by a number of praiseworthy buildings which bore witness not only to the inhabitants piety but also to the ancient city's great wealth.

The wild beauty of the cliff and the surrounding medieval castle which jelously guards the splendour of the ancient monuments behind its towers and thick walls leaves the beholder in awe. Today the acropolis of Lindos is no longer surrounded by the sacred grove which the ancient Lindians tended with such care and piety. Indeed Aglohartos, Athena's priest, at the height of her worship in the 3rd and 4th centuries proudly recorded the care and trouble taken to preserve the ancient grove on several inscriptions. The worship of a female diety on this rocky site dates back to the dim realms of early prehistory. First the Acheans and later the Dorians identified this pre Greek diety with the goddess Athena. Pindar narrates how this ancient temple was founded by the Heliades, the direct descendants of the sun god, and explains the reason for the absence of an altar. To Lindian Athena

Kamiro: General view

they did not offer sacrifices on burning flames. Their offerings were grain, fruit, sweets, liquids and other items which were the product of the earth and which did not require burning. These offerings are referred to by Pindar as "fireless offerings" and traces their origins back to the Heliades. According to legend the Heliades, in their haste to be the first to offer sacrifices to Athena, quickly ascended the cliff forgetting to bring fire with them. This oversight by the Heliades was the source of the fireless offerings. The myth of the Heliades is not the only myth which refers to the founding of this temple. The myth of Danaos, who was the father of the Greek race, is also associated with the temple. According to this myth when Danaos and his daughters fled from Eygpt on their way to the Peloponessus, Danaos stopped at Lindos. During the course of his stay on the island he founded the temple and set up the first statue of the goddess. This statue was a simple peice of unprocessed wood, the symbol associated with a form of worship which is called "xoano" (that is the worship of a wooden image). The first temple dedicated to the goddess was built in the 8th century BC and it was during this century

that the diety was first depicted anthropomorphically. This statue was small in size and made of wood. This archaic temple survived until the time of Kleoboulos. In the 6th century Kleoboulos built a new temple and decorated it and the statue of the goddess with trophies from his numerous victories. The ruins which survive today do not date from the 6th century temple. This was destroyed in 342 BC by a large fire. On the site of the destroyed temple the Lindians built a new temple and the old wooden statue of the diety was replaced by another. This new statue had a wooden body which was gilded and marble head, hands and feet. The history of the temple and a description of the votive offerings are set out in great detail by Timahidas in the chronacles of Lindos. One is impressed not only by the number of votive offerings which are outlined but also by the number of statues which adorned the temple, the plinths of which only survive today.

A little below the temple, at the entrance of the acropolis a large stoa in the Doric order was built in the year 200 BC, while the temple dedicated to Psithirou, the god of prophesy, was built in 200 AD. During the Middle Ages the Byzantines fortified the ancient acropolis by building an im-

The village of Lindos.

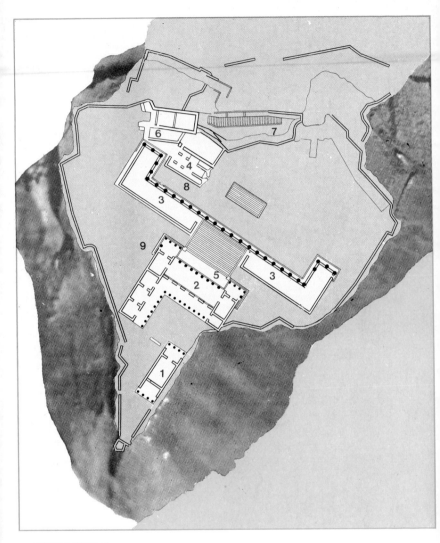

LINDOS CITADEL
1. Temple of Lindia Athena
2. Propylaea
3. Great Arcade
4. Byzantine church
5. Archaic steps
6. Governor's Building
7. Trireme sculptured on the rock
8. Small Reservoir
9. Great Reservoir

pregnable castle and the church of St. John. The successors of the Byzantines, the Knights built another castle which enclosed the surrounding area and the palace of the Keeper of the Castle. One can reach the acropolis along the southern slope of the hill. As soon as one passes through the main gate one finds a stairway which leads to a small square. To the right, carved in the rock of the cliff by Pythourito of Timoharou in 180 BC, one can see an impressive monumental structure made up of a circular exedra in front of which stands a large plinth. This plinth was either the base of an altar or the base of a statue. The stern of a triere can be seen along the side of the exedra. The length of the relief is 4.46m and its height is 5.50m. Many details can be discerned which aid in reconstructing the technical details of ancient shipbuilding. In the same area there are the remains of Byzantine water cisterns and the remains of an archaic stairway. A newer stairway with approximately 80 steps leads up to a domed entrance and the medieval administrative building which was also the home of the Knights' Keeper of the Castle. Passing through the medieval entrance one can see the remains of the Byzantine church dedicated to St. John and the Doric stoa which has been restored and

whose columns have been erected in situ. The stoa is in the shape of a Greek P and measures 90m in length, 8.9m in width and 6.20m in height. There were 42 Doric columns along the facade and 8 Doric columns along its sides. The columns were polygonal one third of their height up while the other two thirds of the columns were fluted. In the centre of this magnificent Hellenistic structure there was a staircase with 36 steps, built on top of the older staircase of Kleoboulos, which led to the Propylaea. The Propylaea was built in the 5th century BC and is a copy of the Propylaea found on the Acropolis of Athens.

On the highest point of the triangular plateau the Lindians built a temple dedicated to their patron goddess. The length of this temple is 22.40m and the width is 7.20m. A dipstyle temple in the Doric order, only sections of its walls have survived intact and several columns have been restored to their original position.

The archaeological area is not limited only to the area of the acropolis, but extends to include the entire surrounding area. Carved out of the western slope of the hill lies the ancient theatre. The orchestra, the platform of the altar and 27 seats survive. Near the theatre stands the church of

Reproduction of the Acropolis of Lindos.

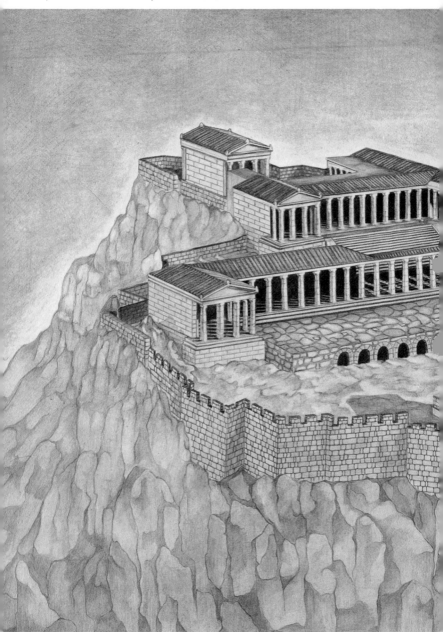

St. Stephen. The large rocks which surround the church are the remains of the wall which enclosed the ancient city's gymnasium. The excavations which were carried out by Danish archaeologists in 1904 revealed not only a great number of inscriptions and artifacts, but also marble slabs which recorded in inscription the history of the temple of Lindian Athena, and found under the ancient floor flagstones of a Byzantine church. This is the now famous Chronicle of Lindos which is today housed in the museum of Copenhagen.

The foundation remains of another temple dedicated to the goddess Athena lie in the position of Vegli, on the northern slope of the hill and facing the large harbour. This temple is the so called ''Boukopion'' temple whose name is derived from the Boukopia sacrifices which were held in Athena's honour. The Dorians built this small temple in the 9th or 10th century BC so that they could offer to the goddess the slaughtered sacrifices which was the decreed custom.

During the Hellenistic Period a large circular structure constructed of large roughly hewn stones was built on the small peninsula which enclosed the bay of Palaistras, the harbour of ancient Lindos. The external perimeter of the monument is 28.42m while its height is 2.80m. The local inhabitants call it the Tomb of Kleoboulos. The main entrance to the interior is gained on the southwestern side. A narrow corridor leads to a small sepulchre chamber. On the southwestern side of the chamber, dug into the rocky ground, lies the tomb of the man in whose honour this monument was built. This structure was also used in later times as a church dedicated to St. Emiliano.

Lindos: The temple of Athena

MUSEUM

The achaeological museum of Rhodes is located in the Museum square in the medieval city. The building which houses the museum is an outstanding architectual structure of the medieval period. The artifacts on display are not limited to those found on the island of Rhodes and include artifacts found on the other Dodecanese Islands. These record all human activity from the Neolithic Period and onwards. The museum is housed in the Hospital of the Knights of the Order of St. John. The building is a two storied structure and is outstanding for its architecture design and decorative.

It was begun in 1440 and completed in 1480. In 1522 the Turks used the building as their barracks. In 1913 the Italians restored the building and turned it into a museum.

Above the building's gothic entrance there is a marble slab carved in relief which depicts two angels holding the Order's coat of arms. Above this relief a small arch projects from the interior of the chapel and three windows which are decorated with medieval motifs.

In the museum's courtyard there is a marble statue of a lion which dates from the Hellenistic Period, post Hellenistic mosaics and countless stone and iron balls. The stone balls are war momentos of the siege of Demetrius the Besieger and the iron balls the momentos left behind by the Turks. A stairway leads up to the first floor of the building. From under a covered stoa one can see the entire floor. A large gate leads to the hospital's great hall. This large room is divided by a series of octagonal columns which are embellished with the coat of arms of the Grand Master Aubusson. The stone slabs on display are the tombs of the Knights from the 14th, 15th and 16th centuries. A sacrophagus which dates from the Classical Period had been used for the tomb of the Grand Master Corneillan. Above the sacrophagus, whose lid is now on display in a French museums, stands the plaster bust of the Grand Master.

The exterior of the Church of the Virgin

Lindos: The church of the Virgin

General view of the Acropolis of Lindos

Old manor house with Lindian plates

An exterior view of the large Doric Stoa

The Temple of Athena on the Acropolis of Lindos

Entrance to the Harbour of the Apostle Paul

Lindos: The Harbour of the Apostle Paul

The beach at Lindos'

The stone ship, carved on the cliff of Lindos' Acropolis

On the southern side of the room stands a medieval fireplace which has been preserved in outstanding condition together with marble reliefs which date from the 2nd century BC. The hospital's small chapel is located along the eastern side of the great hall. The knight who was responsible for the hospital's administration was named Valais and was a member of the French Tongue. Along the walls of the hall there are small openings which lead into small dark rooms whose purpose is unknown.

From the great hall one enters another large room which served as the knights' cooking area and dining room. The fireplace over which most of the cooking was done has been preserved in excellent condition. This room is divided into smaller rooms all of which display artifacts which date from the Archaic, Classical, Hellenistic and Roman Periods. Most of the peices are funerary stelei, some with reliefs others smooth surfaced, Kouroi, and others statues which have been recovered from different islands almost all the islands of the Dodecanese. There are a great number of reliefs depicting various subjects such as Kakabou on horseback, a sacrifice where a child leads the sacrificial animal, a marble urn with the figure of a man and woman carved in relief

flanking the figure of a man on horseback who holds a scarab and looks at a snake which is slowly climbing up a tree. Sepulchre stelei from Nisiro complete the collection on display in the dining hall. The famous funerary stele of **Krito and Timarista** is displayed in the room which has been named after it. This stele comes from Kamiros and has a height of 2m.

It depicts two women, Timarista the deceased and her daughter Krito who tenderly embraces her dead mother. The funerary stele of Kaliaristis dates from the 4th century and was found in the city of Rhodes. Part of a statue of a woman also comes from the city of Rhodes. Of all the pieces from the Archaic period two Kouroi are worth noting which date from the 6th century and which are outstanding examples of Cycladic art in its purest form. Another stele comes from Kamiros as does the anthemion of a funerary stele. In the garden statuary and sepulchre slabstone are also on dispaly. In the room of Aphrodite which is the next successive room, the statue of the goddess, a masterpiece of 3rd century BC art, is on display togeher with the bust of the sun god Helios which dates from the 2nd century BC and is a fine example of Hellenistic craftmanship. The bust was found incorporated into the building materials of a Rhodian house. The figure of a nymph resting against a rock is unfortunately headless as is the statue of a Muse both displayed next to the bust of an athlete. The next room, the room of the **Bathing Aphrodite**, displays a very small statuette of the goddess of beauty washing her hair with delicate fingers while her knee rests on a rock. It is claimed that this small masterpiece is a copy of statue by a Bythian sculptor. The head of Asklepios and the goddess Hygeia are also outstanding pieces. From all the artifacts on display we would like to mention two more, the statue of Zeus and the figure of a satyr who leans against a wine skin. The room was named after the statue of the poet Menandrou on display here. Apart from the figure of the poet there are also sections of the cornice which were recovered from the temple of Erethimou Apollo. The cornice was found in the village of Tholo. Large pithoi and altars which date from the 7th and 6th centuries respectively and found at Ialysos and Kamiro are displayed in a covered stoa of the museum. A rich collection of pottery, ceramic pieces and other smaller artifats are displayed in the remaining rooms of the museum. Black on red, red on black vases cast in the workshops of Rhodes, Attica, Crete, Pheonicia, Asia Minor, and Egypt, all lavishly embellished with motifs drawn from the animal and plant world, are indicative of the sophisticated development the art of pottery achieved from the 10th century BC onwards.

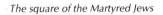
The square of the Martyred Jews

THE CITY OF RHODES

It would not be an overstatement to say that the city of Rhodes is the most interesting city in all of Greece. The entire city is a multifaceted monument. The architecture of this unique city could only have been achieved at the spot where people and cultures came to a juncture. Rhodes was such a place, a crossroad of East and West.

Greeks and western Europeans of the 14th, 15th and 16th centuries, Turks and Italians and once again Greeks helped to develop the modern day city of Rhodes. A city whose urban planning, if not drawn up by the famous Hppodamo, was surely

drawn up according to the city's own inspiration for design.

The lush green north eastern acrotiri of the island was first chosen as the location by the ancient Rhodians to build their city in 408 BC. Perhaps it was the natural harbours which promted the people of Ialysos, Kamiro and Lindos to abandon their own cities and take up residence here for ancient sources refer to more than the three harbours which have survived to the present. The modern harbours were also used by the ancient Rhodians. The small harbour named Mantraki was used more as a military rather than as a commercial harbour. At the mouth of the harbour one can see the chains submerged underwater which closed the mouth off when it was necessary. The larger harbour named Emborio was the main commercial harbour together with the not so significant harbour of Akantias.

The walls which protected the ancient city were strong and stout and were reinforced by the two acropolis, the upper and lower acropolis. The upper acropolis is the present day hill of St. Stephen (Monte Smith) and the lower acropolis is modern day Castello. The harbours were also extensively fortified. The scant remains of the ancient wall do not allow for the reconstruction of their exact position around the city. What is known for certain is that the wall encircled an area of approximately 700 hecates and protected a popluation which, during its highest period of prosperity, reached 50,000 inhabitants.

Wide straight roads cut across the city which was built amphitheatrically, while a near perfect sewage system collected and channelled wastes and rain water. A section of this system dates from 400 BC. All the main roads of the medieval city and those which lead to and from the castle are all roads which date from the ancient city. The famous street of the knights is a street which dates from the 4th century BC.

The high degree of building activity which occured during the period of the Knights destroyed practically all of the ancient buildings. Very few sacred, public and private building survived the building ventures and activities of the Knights, nor have there survived any ancient sources which give detailed descriptions of what the ancient city was like during antiquity. The travel diary of a visitor to the city in 1190, a time when the ancient city had not yet been completely built over, is not sufficient detailed to determine the size of the city.

There are very few archaeological areas in Rhodes and few ancient buildings which have survived. Thus not even a small section of the complex named "Digma" which was composed of a series of buildings and located near the harbour, has survived. This was ancient Rhodes commercial centre, a centre reknown for its beauty. Altars and statues decorated the exterior facades while in the interior halls merchandise was displayed and the Rhodians negotiated and concluded all types of commercial transactions. Nor has anything survived from the ancient agora which was located near the commerical centre, nor of the ancient theatre of Dionysus which was named "Dionysion". Not a trace can be seen of the great temple dedicated to the sun god Helios. The temple of the patron god of Rhodes is believed to have been located near the palace of the Grand Masters. The temple of Aphrodite was located near Symis Square.

A VISIT TO THE NEW CITY

The facade of the new city is adorned with the statues of two deer set high up on columns, Byzantine windmills, the tower of St. Nicholas and the harbour of Mandraki.

At the beginning of this century, the new city of Rhodes was begun beyond the medieval walls. The new city is characterised by its modern urban planning, contemporary market, large hotel complexes, wide streets and beautiful parks. The buildings which were constructed by the Italians in a neo gothic style add a unique and quaint feature to the new city which is most notable in the harbour area. The oldest building which is found in the new city is the tower of St. Nicholas (1464) which marked the end of the medieval fortifications. Less old is the Mosque of Mourat Reis which was built in 1522 and which is located near the Administrative building. The mosque was built on the site of the catholic church dedicated to St. Anthony, and built by Suleiman the Magnificent to honour his admiral, Mourat Reis. This was the official Turkish cemetery and include several truly beautiful tombs of both Viziers and Pashas. The triple domed gothic basilica decorated with interesting wallpaintings by Kondoglou, was built in 1925 and is a faithful reproduction of the medieval church dedicated to St. John of the Knights. It was built by the Italians as a catholic church dedicated to St. John. In 1947 it passed to the Orthodox church and rededicated to the Assumption. Today it is the Metropolis of Rhodes. The building which houses the island's administration is a mixture of Byzantine, Medieval and Spanish architecture. There is a monument located under its wide spanned arch. It was on this very spot on March 31, 1947 that the English military administrator handed over the administration of the Dodecanese to the Greeks. Until the end of World War II the administration of the Dodecanese was excerised by Great Britain who had been appointd by the United Nations.

AQUARIUM

The aquarium of Rhodes is considered to be the finest aquarium in all the Mediterranean. Its 24 water tanks which display the underwater world is not limited to Greek fish species but includes many species of tropical fish as well a several species of water mammals. Seals and sea turtles greet the visitor upon his arrival. A stroll along the Street of the Palm trees is also a must.

Picturesque lane.

ARCHAEOLOGICAL AREAS

MONTE SMITH (The hill of St. Stephens).

On the outskirts of the city, identified as the location of the ancient acropolis, stands Monte Smith. Villas have been built at the foot of this small hill set in a lush green landscape. The view from the peak is absolutely breathtaking. The hill was named after the English Admiral Smith who used the site as a lookout post to keep close watch on Napoleon's fleet during the French war against Egypt.

On the slope of the hill, and now extensively reconstructed by the Italians, stands the stadium which originally dated to the 2nd century BC together with the Small Theatre of ancient Rhodes, also reconstructed. It has been suggested that the small theatre, which holds an audience of 800, was used for the lessons of the Apollonian School of Rhetoric. There was of course another larger theatre, but its exact location is unknown. The gymnasium was located near the small theatre. On the peak of the hill remains from the ancient temple dedicated to Athena Poliados and Zeus Polieos have been discovered. It was in this temple that the Rhodians kept their official state treaties. A little

below the peak there are a series of caves and stoae. Remains which have been found there suggest that this was a sacred place to the nymphs who were probably worshipped here. The scanty remains of columns, foundations and triglyphs suggest that the large temple dedicated to Pythian Apollo was a peristyle Doric temple with metopes and triglyphs. In the large area surrounding the temple several artifacts have been found together with the remains of several buildings. A tomb cut out of the cliff and architectually embellished lies west of the stadium. To the south more tombs were found which suggests that this area may have been a cemetery.

RHODINI. Rhodini, Rhodes public park, is located not far from the centre of the city. Artificial canals and lakes decorated with various plant, a small zoo and many flowers create an idyllic environment which the visitor seeks after his visit to the nearby cemetery.

The cemetery which dates from the 4th and 3rd centuries is located south west of the park.

Among the rock carved tombs one tomb, ''The tomb of Ptolemy'' can be seen. The name is medieval in orgin and has no historical validity. The tomb's shape is square, each side of the base is decorated with Doric pillars and measures 28 meters in length.

Rhodini, the large park outside the city of Rhodes

ARCHAEOLOGY — ARTS — SCIENCES

Archaeological excavations continuously bring to light evidence which dates from as early as the Neolithic Period, when the island of Rhodes was first inhabited, which bear witness to the islanders' activities in all areas of life.

The artifacts from the Neolithic Period are so limited that an extensive study of the period is not possible. A few Neolithic artifacts have been found in the area of Lindos and archaeologists claim that patient research and excavations will eventually yield enough information to reconstruct a full picture of the life of Neolithic man.

Unlike the meagre finds from the Neolithic period, the finds which date to the Bronze Age are numerous. The rich archaeological finds from this later period allow one to formulate a more complete reconstruction of man's society during this period. According to the find, the society which developed during this period was a highly sophisticated one.

The cultural level of the society in Rhodes and their creation of art forms rivalled those of Mycenae. The archaeological artifacts recovered from the Tholos tombs cut into the cliffs on the plateau "Kehraki" near Kamiros are of equal craftsmanship, design and construction equal craftsmanship as the tholos tombs discovered at various sites on Mainland Greece.

The pottery and artifacts which have been recovered from different regions of the eastern Mediterranean (Greece, Egypt, Pheonicia and Asia Minor) indicate that the Rhodians during the pre Greek period were not only cultivators of the fertile land of their island but also skilled sailors and shrewed merchants. Commerce, shipping, olive cultivation, agriculture and livestock as well as the art of pottery were all sources of wealth for the island. The wealth and security allowed the Rhodians to develop intellectual and artisitic activities. The art of this period, indifferent to the design and decorature features of the pottery, drew the pictorial representations from both life on land and in the sea. The indifference shown to pottery shapes gives way c. 1100-1000 BC to a new style which was developed. Severe in the shape and the design of the pottery as well as the decorative motifs depicted. This new style is based almost entirely on geometric shapes and is called "The Geometric Style", a style which is pure Greek in form.

The Geometric Style slowly and steadily received influence from the Middle East, an influence which is fist seen in the pottery of Rhodes 700 BC. This is the "Oriental Period" which replaces the severity of the geometric designs as decorative motifs. Pottery from this period is impressive both in terms of its decorative motifs, colours and delicacy of design. The Oriental style is followed by the Dedalus style which is a mixture of geometric and oriental art. The first great monuments which date from this period are rendered in this style. Pindar states that the statues from this period all seemed lifelike and gave the impression of arrested movement. Unfortunately no large statuary has been found to confirm the written accounts of not only Pindar but of the other great poet, Kalimachos, who lived in the 3rd century BC and who describes at great length the first xoana statue of Hera which was hewn out of unprocessed wood. Several explanations have been put forth by researchers for the absence of large statues one such suggestion is the lack of suitable marble from which the statue could have been carved. Thus Rhodian artists were confined to working metal on wooden images which rarely survive the passage of time. On the other hand many pieces of jewelry of outstanding craftsmanship has been found together with artifacts which confirm the high degree of artistic craftmanship which was attained by Rhodian metallurgists.

Art was not the only thing which flourished on the island of Rhodes. Another area of culture which was highly developed was that of letters. Rhodes offered the perfect environment for the development of intellectual life which was unrivalled and lasted for so many centuries that it became an essential part of the lives of the Rhodians. From the 7th century BC and onwards Rhodes boasted of several worthy intellectuals such as Peisandro from Kamiros. Peisandro narrates in the epic "Herakleia" the mythical adventures of their leader Hercules. Hercule's club and lion skin are first referred to and described in this epic poem by Peisandro. Individual identity of intellect and politics were two characteristics which were demanded from the 6th century BC Tyrant Kleoboulos.

The lyric poet Timokreon was renknown during the period of the Persian Wars. Of his poem "the Timokreonda" only a few verses have survived. The founding of the city of Rhodes in 408 BC provided the island with its intellectual and artistic centre which dominated not only the island but the surrounding areas as well. The founding of Rhodes ushers in a new period of artistic and intellectual creativity. The combined intellectual and artistic forces of Lindos, Ialysos and Kamiro eliminated the barriers of parochial limitations and gave new scope and direction to intellectual and artistic activities. During periods of prosperity Rhodes became the intellectual and cultural centre of the ancient world. Poets, philosophers, architects, sculptors and painters lived and created on Rhodes. These creators were not only native Rhodians but also foreigners who settled on the island of the sun. For many centuries this dominance over the intellectual and artistic affairs was a source of great pride for the inhabitants of Rhodes.

Ancient Greek and foreign artists and scholars felt it necessary to visit Rhodes either as students or as masters. This unrivalled cultural supremacy lasted until the period of Cassius' arrival to the island. It is said that this violent Roman carried off 3000 works of art to Italy. The intellectual culture which flourished on Rhodes from the end of the Bronze age until the Hellenistic Period found its purest expression and created its most breathtaking masterpieces during the

Hellenistic Period. Famous painters, sculptors and architects lived and created on Rhodes eternal works of art, some of which are today scattered throughout the various museums in Europe, other works of art did not survive destruction by the invaders who periodically arrived on the island, while yet other pieces did not withstand the passage of time. The great painter Parrasios, son of the sculptor Eubinorou, lived during the period when the city was founded. Parrasios worked more in Athens than he did on Rhodes. Several of his paintings are found in Lindos. The painting which depicts Hercules, Meleagro and Perseus is found in Rhodes. Other artists included the sculptor Briaxis who lived during the 4th century BC and Lysippos, considered to be the father of Hellenistic art and Deinokratos, the famous architect attached to Alexander the Great. Deinokratos had asked Alexander's permission to carve his likeness out of Mount Athos which is located in the area of Halkidiki in Macedonia. The general did not give his permission for he deemed such an act an insult to the gods and feared that it would bring their displeasure upon him. Protagoras lived and worked on Rhodes as did Chares, the student of the great Lysippos, who

was the creator of the Colossus. **The Colossus of Rhodes** was not the only monumental statue to be created. Colossal was also the famous bronze Tethripou which bore the sun upon it and which was the work of Lysippos. Pliny writes that on Rhodes there were 100 colossal statues which were smaller in size than the statue created by Chares. Any one of these colossal statues would have given great pride to any city which possessed them. Among these statues were the five colossals of Briaxida. Chares' Colossus left a lasting impression on the imagination of the people during the Middle Ages thus giving rise to the various legends of its original location. One such legend claimed that this enormous statue was located over the mouth of the harbour and all ships entering and leaving the harbour sailed between the gigantic statues legs. Today the exact location chosen by Chares for the statue of the sun god Helios is unknown. Yet another famous artistic person of ancient Rhodes was Protogenis. Protogenis came from the city of Kauno in Caries, an area in Asia Minor which was a colony of Rhodes. This great artist lived at the end of the 4th century BC and spent most of his life living and working on the island of Rhodes. He was reknown not only as a

painter but also as a caster of bronze. Apelles, another great artist of antiquity, once conceeded that Protogenis was his equal if not his superior.

Protogenis' most famous work is the painting of the mythical hero and founder of Ialysos. This painting took the artist 7 years to complete while any other contemporary artist (so tradition claims) would have taken 11 years to finish. Equally famous is his painting of a satyr which stands leaning against a column holding a flute in his hand. Protogenis did not produce many paintinop, indeed he was not a prolific artist but he was a perfectionist, for according to legend he spent most of his time reworking his paintings which were never quite to his satisfaction. According to tradition Apelles once criticised him by saying that the artist never knew when to take his hands off the painting. Other well known artists were the painters Simos and Ophelionas whose works are seen in the painting of Aerope, the wife of Atreus and the feast of the Atreids.

Filiskos was yet another sculptor whose talents shone during the 3rd century BC. His works include the Aphrodite and the group of figures depicting Apollo, Artemis, Leto and the Nine Muses. This group of figures was taken to Rome.

Apollonius and Tauriskos originally came from Tralleis in Asia Minor, both reknown sculptors who lived and worked on Rhodes during the 2nd century BC. Their work is the group of statues depicting Dirkis, the Queen of Thebes and the punishment she received at the hands of Zitho and Amphiona, the children of the King of Thebe's first wife Lykou. Today a replica of this work of art can be seen on display in the Museum of Naples, now named "The Farnese Bull".

Agesander, Athinodorus and Polydorus created many sculpted masterpieces during the 1st century BC, the most famous of which is the "Laocoon", a composition which represents Laocoon and his two sons are caught in a fatal embrace by two large snakes. This was the last piece created before Rhodian art began to decline. The most debated question in the history art however is whether the famous **Nike of Samothrace**, which is now in the Louvre Museum, is the masterpiece of a Rhodian artist. This unrivalled masterpiece of Hellenistic art has been attributed to the Rhodian sculptor Pythokritis, the son of Timocharou. Some have suggested that this piece was commissioned in honour of Eudamou's naval victory against Antiochus in 190 BC. An exact date is not given for the statue thus its date an approximation based on the style of the Period. What is known for a fact is that the plinth on which the statue rested is of marble quarried from the island. Artistic development was only one aspect of Rhodian civiliation, the other aspect was the intellectual development. After the foundation of the new city as the arts developed so did intellectual activities. Indeed was such as philosophy, rhetorics, astronomy and generally all aspects of intellectual activity, were developed to such a degree that the island's reputation was the most envied in the area. Local and foreign inhabitants created an intellectual centre which equalled that of Athen's.

Great Aeschines sought refuge here on the island when he left Athens. He was the founder of the school of rhetorics where such notable Rhodian figures as the rhetorics Artamenis, Theodoros, Athinordors and Stasilas taught. The rhetorics who really brought the school to a envied position appeared much later and these masters were all foreigners who had taken up residence on the island. Apollonios and Malakos arrived to the island in 200 BC and soon after were followed by their fellow countryman Apollonios Molon. Their origins were from Asia Minor. Apollonios of Molon followed the prototypes set down by Ipereidi and his pupils numbered among the most important figures of ancient Rome. Julius Caesar and Cicero were only two of his pupils. To these two rhetorics the Rhodians entrusted significant and delicate diplomatic missions, another indication of how highly the islanders viewed their intellectuals.

Philosophy is represented on Rhodes by the Rhodian pupil of Aristotle, Eudimos. Eudimos was a faithful pupil of the master and taught various writings of Aristotle. "The Ethic Narrations" has been attributed to both Eudimos and Aristotle. Eudimos was active in the 4th century BC. Praxiphanis and Ieronimos were the successors to the philosophical school in the 3rd century. The Stoic philosophers Panaetius and Poseidonos further added glory to the school of Philosophy on Rhodes which flourished and reached a peak during the Hellensitic period.

Panaetius the son of Nikagora was the descendent of an old and historic family who achieved greatness as a philosopher. He was born on the island of Rhodes and studied at Pergamon and Athens and lived for many years in Rome. The Athenians offered him the much coveted status of citizen which he turned down claiming that for the truly wise, one country suffices. In Rome he developed close relationships with many intellectual and political figures, at it was during this time that he also met the Greek historian Polybio.

Although a stoic philosopher, Panaetius abandoned many of the older tenets of stoicism and introduced new ideas and attitudes to the philosophical principles of the Stoics.

The establishment of the Mesis Stoa by Panaetius marked a high period in the history of Stoicism. Freed from supertitions, prophesy and astrology, the Stoicism of Panaetius takes the form of rationalism. The world according to Panaetius is unborn, hence indestructable. The soul is not immortal but composed of fire and air. The philosopher accepted the premise that a god existed, a god however who ensured a balanced harmony and order of nature but who did no actively in the life of man. He believed that man being a rational entity could direct nature. To the principles of the older form of stoicism he added discipline of the senses to the will of reason. The ethic ideal is achieved by man not through indifference which was advocated by earlier stoics but through the performance of good deeds which brings about spiritual contentment and satisfaction. This spiritual satisfaction is called "Euthimia" by the philosopher. Panaetius rejected the tenet that all men were equal for he believed in the individuality of man which could not be found in the same form in anyone else. He believed that there existed a relationship between men and the geographical areas they lived in. He claimed that man could not live egocentrically and independerly but that man had to work with his fellowmen for co operation and compromise helped in mankind's development. Two works entitled "On Duty" and "On Happiness" (Euthimia) were written by Panaetius.

Panaetius, the founder of the Mesis Stoa, lived and worked between the years 185 — 110 BC. Poseidonius (135-51 BC) was the pupil who succeeded Panaetius as master and director of the school. He was born in Apamia in Syria and he was considered by some of his admirers to be the last great intellect of ancient Greece. Prior to his residency on

Sunset over the harbour's entrance

The beach a little outside the city of Rhodes

Rhodes in 90 BC the philosopher had visited the most significant intellectual centre of his time either as a student or as a master. In Athens where he spent several years, he succeeded Panaetius as the director of the school of philosophy in 110 BC.

Poseidonius re-introduced the religious aspect into Stoicism and taught that only through virtue could man attain divinity. The soul, according to Poseidonius, came from god but because of a sin committed, it was trapped in the human body. If man could endure the earthly tests he was forced to undergo and live his life virtuously then his soul become worthy to return to god from whence it came. God, according to the philosopher, had no

specific shape or form, but could appear in whatever form he chose. He claimed that the true form of the Diety was a breath of fire which was omnicient and omnipotent. In his book entitled [On the Ocean' although he did not openly acknowledge that the world was spherical, he claimed that if a ship set sail in a westerly direction and had easterly winds behind it, then it would eventually reach the Indies. In the same book he explained that tidal phenomena derived from the moon. Finally the philosopher believed in phrophecy and in mysticism. The development of Greek philosophical thought comes to an end with Poseidonius who was the last great philosopher.

Literature and the literary studies which were developed on Rhodes put the island in the forefront of this field and established it as one of the leading centres during the Hellenistic Period. "The Art of Grammar", a text book used until well into the Renaissance was first written on Rhodes by Dionysios Thraca (170-90 BC). Timahidas of Lindos was another leading figure of history and literature. His only work which has survived is the Chronicle of the Temple of Lindian Athena. This historic chronicle was written on a marble slab in 99 BC. The slab is approx-imately 2.40 x 0.85. Upon this slab Timahida wrote the history of the goddess Athena's temple at Lindos. This marble inscribed slab in today displayed in the Museum of Copenhagen. Poetry is represented by Simias and Apollonios. Simias acheived fame for his lyric poetry and em-pigrams. Apollonios, although not a native of Rhodes, is known in history as Apollonios the Rho-dian because he lived on the island for many years. Of all his literary works the only one which has survived is the epic poem en-titled "The Argonautics", a fine example of Hellenistic poetry. The poem is distinguished for its burning passion and complex tone.

Lastly the mathematician and astrologer Ipparchos was yet another figure who lived on Rhodes and who made his first astrological observation in 161 BC.

The Hellenistic Period is the period which brought art in all its forms to their peak and where thought was developed to the highest degree. During the Roman Period the decline of the arts and learning began and steadily the need for spiritual ex-pression of the mind and the arts dwindled. Spontaneous creativi-ty gave way slowly and steadily to mimicry and replica and the moment of decline had arrived, a decline which was to last for centuries but which did not erase Rhodian art's source of artistic intuition and inspiration.

Centuries later the Rhodian creator will express a new art-form – that of secred or Christian art.

THE MIDDLE YEARS

The decline of intellectual and artistic activities mark the end of the ancient world. This end however did not erase the intellectual and artistic tradition which had lasted for so many centuries. This tradition was maintained by the anonymous Rhodian artist. Although the great men of the past were not succeeded during the period of decline in the artistic and intellectual fields a small group of anonymous Rhodian artists continued to produce their creations based on the old traditions but incorporting a new expression in their work. An expression of the needs and insecurities of the times. The medieval creator drew inspiration from the long artistic tradition, a tradition which was evident in the old christian monuments of the island. Today a large number of Paleo Christian churches have been discovered on the island. Most of these churches were basilicas and some of them are noted for their highly artistic baptistries and baptistry fonts. A

great number of sculpted architectual pieces such as cornices have been recovered together with episcopal thrones and marble iconostasis. Sacred art is not the only art form which was revived during this period. A new art form developed to meet the defensive needs of the people which served their everyday needs. Examples of this fortification art which was developed during the Byzantine Period are the numerous remains of Byzantine castles and fortresses which are scattered throughout the island.

Architecture and decorative design was further modified during the period of the Knights stay on the island. It is this architectual and decorative style which has survived and which is seen in the monuments which date from this period.

The appearance and development of pottery making was marked very early in the period. The pottery workshops of Rhodes are well known in the Imperial capital as early as the 6th century AD. At first the medieval Rhodian pottery maker copied Persian design and decorative motifs, but within a short period of time he had abandoned the art of copying and became the inspired creator. Characteristics of this newly revived Rhodian art form are the delicate colours and rich variations of decorative motifs. The steady development of pottery making gave rise to the famous "Rhodian Plates" or the "Plates of Lindos" in the 16th and 17th centuries. Both are noted for their rich and colourful designs.

Not only are the arts revived during the period but one can discern a intellectual revival as well. Rhodian man was inspired and he created according to the needs of his everyday life. A new type of poetry is developed which is called the Demotic. An example of this form of poetry is the erotic songs entitled "Words of love and passion". This manuscript dates from the 15th century and is now on display in the Museum in London. Demotic poetry is the poetry of the anonymous popular poet, a man of the people who feet the need to express his emotions in meter form. A need to express his emotions was also felt by the scholar. The impetus which the scholarly Rhodian gave to the intellectual renaissance of his native homeland was exceptional. The contribution of Constantine of Lindos, known as Constantine the Rhodian, was significant in that it broke the parochial boundaries and re-established the name of his native country as a centre of thought among the circles of scholars in the Imperial capital. Born in Lindos in the 10th century, Constantine continued his studies in the state capital of Constantinople. A cleric in the court of the Emperor Constantine the Porphirogenitou, Constantine described in iambic meter the Chruch of the Apostles in Constantinople, a magnificent church which has not survive. The scholar Emmanuel Georgilas who lived during the 15th century left two works of poetry entitled ''The Fatality of Rhodes'', wherein he describes the great plague which ravished his country in 1498-1499, and ''The historical explanation of Velisarius'' which is exemplary of Byzantine fiction in meter form.

The scholarly contribution does not end with the works of these two Rhodians The intellectual development which was revived on the island continued and did not end until the conquest of the Turks in 1522. A new revival in intellectual and artistic activities was seen again in the twentieth century, the century which gave back to Rhodes its intellectual and artistic identity.

RELIGION

The Rhodians were pious Dorians, close to the Doric dieties and worshipped the twelve Greek gods together with Athena and the sun god Helios.

The god Helios, a pre Greek diety, was worshipped in several areas of Greece and was said to be the son of the Titan Hperiona. His siblings were Ious and Selinis. Very little is known as to the worship of the sun god. What is known is that the temples of this pre Greek god were built on hill tops and mountain peaks and that he was offered as sacrifice white horses.

On Rhodes the sun god was worshipped as the main diety. In the city of Rhodes a maginificent temple was built and dedicated to him on the site of an older sanctuary and every four years the Rhodians celebrated a great festival in honour of their patron god which was called ''The Great Aliea''. The festival included not only sacrifices and other ceremonies of worship but also games. The victors received as a trophy of their victory a wreath made of a poplar branch, the sacred tree of the sun god. Apart from this festival the Rhodians also honour their patron god with a festival which was named ''The Minor Aliea''. This festival was held annually and among the items offered to the god was a chariot drawn by four white horses which was driven into the sea. The origin of this sacrifice lay in the belief that the sun god rose from the sea and drove his chariot, which was driven by four white horse, across the heavens.

The goddess Athena was worshipped by the people of Lindos the city where her great temple stood. A celebrated festival was held by the people of the island to honour the goddess of wisdom.

Festivals which honoured the god Apollo, the diety of the Dorians, were also held on the island. The famous festival of Iakinthia, dedicated to Apollo and his brother Iakinthos, did not loose any of the former glory of the Dorian inhabitants of Rhodes. Another god which was devoutly honoured was the protective god of herds, Karneio Apollo, who was honoured during the festival of the Karneia.

Feasts were also held in honour of Hercules, the mythical hero of the Dorians. According to mythology Hercules was the father of Tlipolemou, the leader of the first Doric settlers to arrive on the island.

The feast of Smynthia was dedicated to Smynthio Dionysus where theatrical performances were held in his honour.

During these festivals the Rhodians organized games and contests in athletics, music, theatre and chariot racing. For the major festivals such as the Great Aliea, the Karneia and the festival held in honour of Lindian Athena, offical embassies representing different cities in Greece and surrounding areas arrived to the island. Religious piety was devoutly upheld by the Rhodians, a piety which often served the expediency of the other Greeks.

Christianity quickly spread on Rhodes. Paul, the Apostle of all nations, founded the first Christian church, and from the 1st century onwards Rhodes has been an episcopal seat.

The Government building

THE OLD CITY (CHORA)

Even though a large section of the city has been transformed into a tourist market, the walled city has still retained its medieval colour and character. A stroll along the flagstoned streets leaves the visitor breathless. The houses still retain their original medieval facades beside narrow picturesque arch covered streets. Additional Turkish architectural features, trellis windows, loggias, and minarets present a mixed architectual style never seen before anywhere, for nowhere else in the world did the Gothic, Byzantine and Turkish cultures meet to create this unusual expression of structure and design. On Rhodes where these three cultures met, a city was built which is now the old city of Rhodes.

The mosques show a balance and harmony between the Gothic, Byzantine and Turkish features, for most of the mosques were originally Orthodox chur-

ches which were converted to Catholic churches by the knights before passing to the Turks who turned them into mosques.

Socratous street is a large medieval road which is the city's central street and which divides the old city from the Kastello. It runs into the market centre and the square of Ippocratous where the Castellania is located, a fine example of a 16th century building. This was the medieval Basilica Mercatorum which was later converted into a mosque and was once a commercial seat administered by the knight Bailou. Knight Bailou sat in judgement of all commercial transactions which were disputed. The building is a 16th century example of gothic architecture decorated with the arms of the Grand Masters D'Amboiser and Adam.

The mosque of Suleiman is located in the Byzantine church of the Apostles and is located in the Square of Suleiman.

The mosque was built by the Sultan Suleiman the Magnificent in commemoration of his victory. The building which stands today is 19th century. In the garden there is a 16th century fountain.

An example of Turkish architecture of the last century (1851) is the three storied tower of "Pologiou" which was built on the site of a medieval guard

tower. The clock is a gift of Tahti Pasha, the son of Havous Ahmet Aga, given to the Turks of Rhodes during his visit to the island.

Across from the Mosque of Suleiman stands the Turkish library. This library was founded by Havour Ahment Aga in 1794

A view of the old city

in commemoration of his visit to Rhodes. The library houses several fine manuscripts.

In Apolloniou street where the Byzantine church of St. George once was, in a 12th century building now stands the Mosque Medresse. The church of St. George was given over to the Franciscians in 1457. After 1522 it became a mosque which belonged to the Turkish school of theology in Rhodes. The building is of exceptional beauty and is embellished with 4 lovely apses and a garden.

To the right of Ippocratou square stands the small mosque of Aga. This mosque was built in 1820. On the left side of Agios Phanourios Street stands the Kavlouki Metali Mosque. The Mosque Moustapha was built in 1756 together with the baths of Suleiman which has a dome over the central chamber and whose floors are layed with ancient marble slabs. The baths are located in Zenonos Street.

Behind the Church of St. Phanourio—Aga Mosque stands the Rezep Pasha mosque which is considered to be one of the most significant Turkish buildings in the city. Ancient columns, Byzantine and Medieval features were all incorporated into the building by the Turks.

The Demirli Mosque is located in a side street off of Agios Phanourios (Platonus). Its high dome and 16 pillars which support the round tympanum and four windows makes this mosque the largest Byzantine church in the city dedicated to the Virgin. The church was also used by the Knights.

Another building which is also a fine example of Gothic architecture is the ''Admiralty'' which is located in Aristotelous street (The square of the Jewish Martyrs or the Square of the Archbishopric). This beautiful 15th century building is also known as the ''Archbishopric Megaron''. It has been suggested that this was the residence of either the Catholic bishop or the orthodox Metropolite.

Another old Byzantine church which was later converted into a mosque is the Mosque Dolapli, located in Demosthenous street. The mosque of Il Myhram is located in Pericleous street. The building is a 14th century Byzantine church. Under layers of white plaster and paint one can just discern the remains of the Byzantine wallpaintings.

At the beginning of Pindar street one can see the ruins of St. Katherine's hospital. This hospital was built in the 14th century and restored in the 16th century and was originally founded by the Italian Admiral of the Knights, D'Allemagna. The building was used more as an inn for official visitors rather than a hospital. At the corner of Pindar and Aeolou stands the church of St. Pande-leimonas and next to its walls are the ruins of the church dedicated to "the Virgin of Victory". The church was built after the siege of 1480 to commemorate the Knights' victory against the Turks.

To the left of the church is the Gate of St. Katherine which leads to the area between the commercial harbour and the harbour of the Akantias jetty. This jetty is called "Pier of the Windmills" named after the many windmills located there. On the edge of the pier stands the strongly fortified Tower of the Windmills or The Tower of the Angels.

The harbour road which is much frequented leads to the gate of the harbour.

A VISIT TO KASTELLO OR KOLLAKIO

Passing through the Gate of Freedom and the area of Man-traki where to the righ stands the jetty with its windmills and the Tower of St. Nicholas we find ourselved in the city of the Knights of the Order of St. John. The large palace of the Grand Master, the remains of the Tongues' inns (each ethnic group

The stronghold of St. Nicolas.

Ippocratous Square

had its own Tongue), the arsenal, the hospital and other buildings transport the visitor, as far as contemporary life of the city allows, to the heroic age of the Order. The Gate of Freedom is not a medieval structure, it was opened by the Italians who also cleared the whole area leading to the gate.

In Simis Square behind the ruins of the temple of Aphrodite, a temple built in the 3rd century BC, stands the bulky remains of the Tongue of the Auvergne. The covered stoa and the exterior stairway are all that remain of the building which was completed in 1507. Perhaps behind the cypress trees lies the ancient theatre of Dionysus.

The building that follows and which today houses the National Gallery is the "Armoury" or the "Arsenal" of the Knights. The facade and plan indicates that it was originally the Order's hospital. The building is embellished with the coats of arms of the Grand Masters De Rins (1355-1365) and Caretto (1513-1512).

The medieval building which stands in the square of Argyro-

castro houses the "Museum of Folk Art". The collection is made up of rich local costumes, Rhodian plates and other items of Rhodian art.

The famous Road of the Kinght is located through an archway immediately to the right and across the road to the left is the Enderoum Mosque. This mosque was originally a 12th century Byzantine church. In the 15th century the Knights converted into into a catholic church and dedicated it to the Virgin of Victory. After the island's conquest by the Turks it was converted to a mosque.

Museum square is located right after the church-mosque. East of the square stands the Tongue of England which was restored in 1919. The building presently standing is a faithful reproduction of the original structure which was built in 1483. The Knights' hospital stands on the western side of the square and is one of the most outstanding architectual examples which

Mandraki: The New Market

stands in the city of the Knights. The Archaeological Museum is housed here.

THE ROAD OF THE KNIGHTS:

The entire length of the cobbled road is a medieval accomplishment which serves as a bold monument for its outstanding purity. The medieval road which runs along a straight axis follows an ancient road in the city of Rhodes which began in the harbour and ended at the acropolis. The ancient remains which were found suffice to establish the true age of the road. The road today has a length of 200 m and a width of 6m. During the Middle Ages it most probably began in the harbour and ended at the highest point of the lower city's castle where the palace of the Grand Masters and the church of St. John are today.

The medieval facades of the houses and the emblems of the different tongues and orders are of the purest gothic style which is seen only in medieval cities of

A view of the Knights' Hospital

the West. The entire area to the left, where the road begins, is taken up by the facade of the Hospital-Museum. Next to this buildings stand two buildings, one of which has a very beautiful window. Next to these two building along the right side of the road stands the Tongue of Italy. In the centre of the window on the first floor the coat of arms of the Grand Master Carretto can be seen. The building is not the origninal building of 1519 but a restoration which was carried out by the Italians in 1915. Next to a small and anonymous building, decorated with the coat of arms of the Grand Masters Amboise and Adam and the dates 1510 and 1521 stands the dignified sertains of what was originally the Tongue of France. The heraldic arms of France are set into the facade (lillies and the crown) together with the coat of arms and the relief of D'Ambusson. The relief depicts a cardinal's hat and the date 1495. As well there is the coat of arms of Amboise and the year 1492 which was the year the Inn was completed. The decorative features are all gothic and the upper section and roof resembled the finishings of a crenellated castle while the water sprouts are rendered in the form of crocodile heads. The figures were intended to serve as a reminder to the knights of the Grand Master Gozon who killed a crocodile found in the surrounding area of the city. This act has now become one of the many Rhodian legends. The small palace which stands directly opposite was built in the Spanish style. A small road whose length is covered by arches leads to the small gothic church of St. Demetrius. The church was built in 1499 by the Order's Admiral Piossasko. An ancient inscription found in the church's floor has given rise to the speculation that this church may have been built on the site of an ancient temple dedicated to Dionysus. Back on the Road of the Knights to the left stands a gothic church with an arched door and a corniced niche which holds a statue of the Virgin. It is decorated with the arms and shields of France, England, the Pope and the Grand Masters. The church was most likely built in 1365. After 1522 it was converted into a mosque.

Next to this church stands a building with a very simple facade. Perhaps the residence of an ecclesiastic. An arch which has one room above it and then the Inn of the Tongue of Provence. After the destruction of 1855 the Inn lost part of its original height. Decorative features

The road of the knights.

of the facade are its large gothic door and the coat of arms of Carretto and Flotta.

The arch divided the central room into two unequal chambers of the grand Inn of the Tongue of Spain. The Inn was begun by the Grand Master Fluvian (1421-1437) and completed by D'Amboise (1503-1512) and is decorated with the coat of arms of these two Grand Masters. Certain architectual details create a strong impression of Spain. At the end of the road of the Knights, in the square of Kleoboulos stands the loggia of St. John, a building which was erected much later and bears no relationship with the Middle Ages. The loggia was built on the site of the church of St. John, the patron saint of the Order. The church was built in the 14th century and survived as a mosque until 1856. In the basement of the church someone had at one time stored a large amount of gunpowder. In 1856 lightning struck the church's minaret and seconds later an explosion occured. The church was litterly blown away, the palace of the Grand Masters was destroyed,

Nautical-Gate.

The Liberty-Gate.

but the worst was the death of 800 people.

This explosion and the destructive earthquake of 1851 reduced the palace of the Grand Masters to rubble. This bright building of the 14th century was restored to its present form by the orders of the Italian director De Vechhi during the decade of 1930-1940. A structure imposing both in its dimensions, which are 75m x 80 m, and the strength of its fortifications, it resembles a bastion on the southwestern corner of the castle. The lower section of its external walls, the entrance which faces the square of St. John and a few sections of the northeastern side are all that remain of the original medieval structure. The entire building, apart from its exterior appearance, is the work of unbridled imagination of the Italian architects and decorators of pre world war I.

A grand entrance flanked by two towers complete with embrasures leads into the marble laid courtyard with its stoae and the statues of the Roman Emperors brought over from the island of Kos. The entrances of the underground storerooms can be discerned. A staircase which leads to the upper floor begins at the entrance hall. The rooms in the upper floor are decorated with ancient columns and capitals, ancient, Early Christian and Byzantine mosaics which were brought here from all the islands of the Dodecanese. The furniture of the room is 14th, 15th and 16th centuries. The function, use and decoration of the 90 rooms bear no resemblence to medieval plan, function, use or decoration. These rooms were randomly created by the pre war Italians. A semi circular arch is found in the southwestern corner of the palace which is the canon gate together with the castle's embrasures and the tomb and coat of arms of the Grand Master De Lastic. The surviving section of the wall once separated the Kastello from the city during the period of the Knights. A little below and traversing the wall is the gate of St. Anthony, which was present before the walls were erected and the gate of D'Amroise was built. The gate of St. Anthony and the gate of the embrasure of the Elion were the only gates which gave direct entrance to and exit from the city.

A VISIT TO THE CASTLE

This historic castle, with its unusual square shape whose sides are four kilometers in length and surrounds the city of Rhodes, has never ceased to be an object of awe and admiration. This admiration is derived not only from its fortified perfection but also from its outstanding artistic conception. The artistic value lies in its harmony between the old and the new, a harmony which is best seen in its reliefs, doors and the letters of the inscriptions.

The castle's form as developed after the siege of 1480 is indicative of the Knight's desperate attempt to modify it so that it served their needs and the function for which it was created. The experience of a series of wars taught the Knights that the original thin, high walls could not withstand the attack of small heavy metal canon balls. The well restored old Byzantine castle was radically renovated to fulfill the new conditions of the time.

The Grand Master D'Aubusson, whom the pope created cardinal after his victory over Mohammad II, began this enormous undertaking to modernise the castle. D'Aubusson's endevours were continued by his successors, the Grand Masters D'Amboise and Del Carretto.

After the earthquake of 1481 work on the modernisation of the castle was quickened. The structure which had been badly damaged by the siege and later by the earthquake was quickly transformed into a magnificent castle. The walls' height was lessened while the width, which originally was no more than 2 meters, was increased to 12 meters, in some areas the width exceeds 12 meters. A new tower was built and the weak areas were reinforced with a double wall. The embrasures and battlements were modified to suit the needs of arms both large and small. Large external walkways were created which did not hinder the movement of the defenders. The width of the moat was increased, in areas of greater weakness to as much as 50 meters while its depth was also increased from 16 meters to 23 meters. Particular attention was paid to the design of the fortress' castle gates which were decorated with the Order's coat of arms, together with the coat of arms of the Grand Masters.

Catholic and Orthodox, European and Greek engineers for fourty years attempted to raise a barrier against the Arab invading hordes of the 16th century. Invasions which brought the Turkish Sultan Suleiman II, the Magnificent up to the walls of Vienna.

123

The proud castle withstood the attacks of the soldiers of Islam. They could not, however, withstand an attack based on treason and betrayal.

The visit to the famous castle of Rhodes is a memorable stroll filled with images of the approximately 150 coats of arms of the Order and the Grand Masters, the impressive reliefs incorporated into the maginificent towers and the awe inspiring castle gates. Sections were assigned to each knight during a military campaign. Each nationality or Tongue had its assigned area of the castle to protect.

The most impressive gate is that of D'Amboise which was built in 1512 by the Grand Master D'Amboise and decorated with Order's coat of arms along side the Grand Master's. It is flanked by two towers whose foundations stand at the bottom of the moat. The embrasures of the Palace of the Grand Masters is decorated with the arms of the Grand Master Caretto (1513-1521). The protection of the area from the gate of D'Amboise to the tower of St. George was assigned to the Tongue of Germany. The areas of the rampart was transformed into storage rooms for ammunition. A relief of St. George, the coat of arms of Pope Martin V, the Order and the Grand Master Fluvian are all decorative features of the old castle, the castle which was reinforced by D'Amboise and De l'Adam. The area which was assigned to the Tongue of Auvergne was fortified with a wall which exceeds 12 meters in width and which begins at the tower of St. George and ends at the tower of Spain. The fortifications of the area assigned to Auvergne were works of D'Amboise and Delastic. The tower of Spain is circular and exceeds the height of the walls, surrounded by a four sided battlement which has the arms of the Grand Master Lastic incorporated in its side as a decorative feature. The Tongue of Spain was responsible for the defense of the area which lay between the Tower and the Church of the Virgin. The betrayal which occured during the siege of 1522 occured in this area. The Tongue of England guarded the area which began with the Tower of the Virgin and ended at the Gate of St. John or the Gate Koskinou. The gate was built in 1441 by the Grand Master De Lastic and it is his coat of arms together with a relief of the Virgin which are incorporated into the masonry. The Tower is defended by a wide moat and polygonal battlements with embrasures. The Gate of St.

The entrance of the Grand Masters Palace

Athanasios was protected by the Tower of the Virgin. The name was derived from a relief of St. John which is incorporated into the wall. Its medieval name is Porta Koskinou. The Tongue of Provence was assign to defend the area between this gate and the fortress of Italy. The gate was built by the Grand Master Amboisen and set before much older gates of the castle. The decorative features of this defensive position are the coat of arms of the Grand Masters Fluvian of Lacost and De Milly together with a bilingual inscription (Greek and Italian) which bears the date of August 20, 1512 and records the name of the master builder. The Tower of Italy is very imposing. Its diameter is 50m with a 15 meter wide battlement equipped with embrasures and other fortification features. The coat of arms of the Grand Master Carretto is incorporated into the masonry. The Tongue of Italy was assigned to guard the area between this tower and the Gate of St. Katherine. From the Gate of St. Katherines to Naillac's moat was the are protected by the Tongue of Castile. The main harbour gate was the responsibility of the Castellians. It was built by D'Ambusson in 1478 and is flanked by two lovely towers located above the domed entrance which is Gothic in style

and is decorated with the central figures of the Virgin and Child flanked by the figure of St. John to the right and St. Peter to the left and the coat of arms of the Grand Master D'Aubusson, France and the Order. The Tower of St. Paul stands a little to the north. The Tongue of France was assigned the defense of the area which lay between the Tower of Naillac or the Arabs and the Gate of D'Aubusson. The Tower of Naillac was destroyed by the earthquake of 1863. The Gates found in this area of the castle are all decorated with the coat of arms of the Order, the Grand Master and Pope Sixtus.

Apart from the castle the harbour is also fortied with fortifications which are an extension of the main castle. This is the castle of St. Nicholas which protects the Mandraki Harbour, the military harbour not only of the Knights but of the ancient Rhodians as well. The castle of St. Nicholas stands on the pier of the windmills. Today only three windmills have survived.

The large inner courtyard of the palace

The Gate of Amboise

The Gate of St. John

GENERAL INFORMATION

Rhodes is an island with a tradition of tourism which generously offers the visitor the joys of nature, shopping, the sea, sports, night entertainment and fortune for those who pursue lady luck at the casino.

ACCOMODATIONS

Hotels of all classes, pensions, and rented rooms are not sufficient in number to meet the ever increasing needs of the visitor. It is advisable that before one arrives on the island they should have accomodiations settled. There is a stong possiblity that the visitor may not find anything. If this happens then the best thing to do is consult the police.

FOOD

The restaurants serve not only Greek dishes but also foreign dishes as well. Many restaurants and hotels have modified their cuisine to suit the needs and tastes of the visitor.

The Apostle Paul-Gate.

SERVICES

Post offices, Telephone centres (OTE) National Tourism offices (EOT) and banks can be found not only in the city of Rhodes but in smaller towns and villages on the island.

LOCAL TRANSPORTATION

A very well developed road network connects the city of Rhodes with the island's interior.

Local buses (KTEL) have daily bus schedules which allow for access to all the villages on the island. Apart from public tran-sportation there are also many car and motorcycle rental of-fices. Leading car rental offices such as Heitz and Avis Ban have offices in the city of Rhodes.

THE MARKET OF RHODES

A stroll through the market of Rhodes is a pleasant pastime even for someone who doesn't want to shop. A large cheeful group of people who speak all the European languages help to create this carefree and tranquil atmosphere. The plethora of shops offer a wide selection of items which can satisfy even the

A room of the palace

most demanding of shoppers. An unique tone is given by the objects on sale which range from small inexpensive souvenirs to costly furs and jewels.

SPORTS

For those who love watersports, the beautiful beaches of Rhodes offer all the water sports imaginable. From simple swimming to polo and underwater fishing. Fishing with a net or hook as well as underwater spear fishing require a permit from the harbour authorities. The permit is issued after a requisite form has been completed.

In the area of the city of Rhodes one can swim and participate in a number of water sports.

Swimming

A large beach which is fully equipped and well organised stretches out to the left and right of the aquarium. This beach is well equipped to make a long stay on the beach a pleasurable pastime. Dressing rooms, showers, refreshment stands and cantines which serve fast food, windsurfing and water skiing as well as rented boats with or without engined, canoes and pedallos are available. Apart from this large and organised beach there are several free beaches for those who want to enjoy the sun and water and have no need of organized facilities and services.

Other Water sports

Apart from the Naval Club of Rhodes which offers every possible service and help for those who enjoy water sports, there are private offices which rent all the requisite equipment for all types of water sports. Thus anyone who wants can rent a wind surf, motorboat, water skis, canoes, boats with or without engines as well as the equipment needed for underwater fishing.

There are also basket ball, tennis, golf and other sports offered at either the public or private facilities on the island. The riding club offers the enjoyment of an excursion on horseback.

NIGHT LIFE

A cosmopolitan centre such as Rhodes cannot possibly lack in nightly entertainment. For those who pursue lady luck there is the casino. For those who love to dance there are the large dance halls in the hotels and the various dance clubs. Pubs, Bars, variety features and of course clubs which feature the bouzouki. At

View of the New Market at night

many clubs either dance clubs or musical clubs usually entertain the visitor during intermissions with a group of traditional Greek dancers accompanied by the demotic music.

Theatrical performances, exhibitions of popular art such as the Folklore theatre etc. offer evenings full of pleasant entertainment.

LOCAL FESTIVALS

Aside from the Sound and Light show which is held each year from April until October in the castle's garden there are several local festivals which occur. In September there is a local festival which features tradition dances of the Dodecanese which are performed outdoors. Several festivals are also held throughout the summer in the old city, the National Theatre and the ancient theatre. These festivals include theatrical performances, traditional demotic dances and songs as well as concerts.

FIRST AID

In the event of an accident or illness there following medical facilites are available. The General Hospital in the city of Rhodes and IKA medical offices as well as private clinics and offices.

THE INTERIOR
OF THE ISLAND

Two major motorways, one which leads to the eastern side of the island and the other which leads to the western side, together with their secondary roads ensures easy and comfortable movement from the city of Rhodes to the island's interior.

The beautiful villages, the valleys and the plains, the ancient cities, the medieval castles, the Byzantine churches and chapels all charm and excite the visitor with their simplicity and beauty. Equally exciting is the exploration of the non tourist Rhodes which is located in the southern area of the island. One can come to know the real life of Rhodes and its true beauty in the mountainous villages on the island.

The two major motorways run along the coast of the island and which connect the village of Kattabia with the southern section of the island.

During the drive one can stop and enjoy the clear clean sea at one the many wonderful beaches which are found along the eastern and western coasts of the island.

A meeting with the local cuisine

Dancers wearing the traditional dress

Hand woven textiles

133

WESTERN SIDE OF THE ISLAND

Following the western coastal motorway one comes across the small village of **KRITIKA** a few kilometers out of the city. The name of the village was given by the Turks from Crete who settled in the area in 1898.

To the right the Gulf of Trianda stretches out and 8 kilometers from Rhodes one reaches **TRIANDA** or **IALYSOS** as the natives call it. The village is located very near the sea. The area is lush and overflows gardens and cultivated fields. Here one can see the beautiful stone houses, the so called "Towers" which are old summer homes of the wealthy Rhodians. There are neo classical buildings in the village. From the city of Rhodes to the village the area which lies between is spotted with large hotel complexes. Half of the hotels on the island are located here along this area of the coast which measures 10 kilometers in length. The church of the Virgin, an 18th century bulding, is located in this village. The iconostasis is older. The church dedicated to St. George Christou has wall paintings which date from the 14th and

The village of Trianda (Ialissos).

15th centuries. The monastery of Phaneromenis is located not far from the village. The monastery of the Taxiarchon is located near the village of Kandili, just to the east of the village.

Swimming

The village's beach is covered with pebbles and has a shower and dressing rooms. The beach which runs from the village of Kremasti to the city of Rhodes is ideal for swimming and water sports.

Food and local festivals

A great number of taverns, restaurants, pizza houses, pubs, bars, etc can be found in the village. The local festivals of the village are limited to religious feasts such as the feast of the assumption on August 15th and the feast of Zoodohou Pigi. These festivals are celebrated with local dances and songs.

First Aid

There is a state doctor's office as well as a pharmacy in the village.

KREMASTI

The village is located approximately 12 kilometers from the ci-

The Valley of the Butterflies

ty of Rhodes. A lush green tourist village, it has a number of new houses and is 1000 meters from the sea. An old church and the ruins of an old Venetian castle make up the sights of this village. To the left of the main road at the entrance of the village, an asphalt side road leads to the villages of Pastida and Maritsa.

Swimming

As on all the beaches which lie on the northern coast of the island, the beach here is not very calm, not even during the summer. Apart from the free beach there is also an organized beach with dressing rooms, showers and refreshment stands located here. Along the shore which is covered with green plants up to the shoreline, one can find taverns, restaurants and bars.

Local festivals

A major festival is held here on August 15th. The festival begins on the 14th of August and lasts until the 23rd of August.

First Aid

A medical office and a pharmacy are available here.

Services

OTE (Telephone) There are car service station and taxis available here. Between the village of Kremasti and the Valley of the Butterflies, a distance of 26 kilometers from the city, one comes across the villages of PARADEISI, DIMITRA and KA-LAMONAS. The new airport is located in the area of Paradeisi. The major sight of the village is the church of St. John and its wall paintings. The village of Damatria owes its name to the ancient temple which was dedicated to the goddess Dimitra.

BUTTERFLIES

Three kilometers after the village of Paradeisi and left of the central motorway lies the small fertile valley of the butterflies. The valley is a vision of beauty with its ascending pathways, the small lakes wooden bridges and the trickling water streams. This picturesque, long, narrow and ascending valley was chosen by its inhabitants — the one million butterflies. From June through to September these multi coloured butterflies offer a lovely sight for whoever chosen to disturb their tranquility for just a moment.

Hidden in the foliage of the trees, they rise up like a multi coloured cloud at a clap or some other slight noise. One of the pressing questions which entonomologists have difficulty answering is why this valley is chosen to collect such a vast number of butterflies. Perhaps the valleys plants and foliage are the reasons for the collection of these truly beautful insects. A little above the valley lies the monastery of The Virgin Kalipetras. The monastery was built in 1782 by the Greek potentate of Vlahias (Today an area of Rumania) Alexander Ipsilantis. After a visit to the picturesque valley and perhaps the monastery one returns to the main motorway. 2.5 kilometers along the road one meets the lovely village of **THOLOS or THEOLOGOS.** The village is located 22 kilometers from the city of Rhodes. Along the wonderful beach there are a number of hotel complexes, restaurants, taverns and bars. The ruins of the ancient temple dedicated to Erethimio Apollo are found near the village.

Swimming

The beach offer all types of water sports.

SORONI

The village of Soroni is located 24 kilometers from the city of Rhodes and 4 kilometers from the village stands the monastery of Agia Soula. The festival which is held here on July 30 in honour of the saint is reknown throughout the island. Apart from the food and drink the festival features dances and songs as well as horse and donkey races. Many people come to see the donkey and horse races.

KALAVARDA

The village is located 30 kilometers from the city of Rhodes. Here the motorway branches into a fork. To the left the road leads to the villages of Salako, Apollona and the monastery of the Prophet Ilias. The main road continues on to ancient Kamiro.

SALAKO

This worthy village is located approximately 50 kilometers from the city of Rhodes. Built on the slope of the mountain of Prophet Ilias, the climate is healthy, the landscape a lush green and plenty of flowing water. This is a beautiful example of mountainous Rhodes. The village has restaurants and taverns which meet the needs of the many visitors who come here.

First Aid

A medical office.

PROPHET ILIAS

The monastery of the Prophet Ilias nestles on the peak of the mountain, 15 kilometers from the village of Salako. The cottages which were built in the Tylolean cottage style are worthy of admiration. The hotel "Elafos kai Elafini" (The buck and the roe) is located near the monastery.

Local festivals

Thousands ofp pilgrims arrive to celebrate the feast of the monastery which is held every July 20. The pilgrims climb up the mountain to honour the memory of the Prophet Ilias. Festivals are also held on August 15th and April 23rd, the feast of St. George. One can return to the main motorway from the village of Salako and after a 10 kilometer drive, the archaeological site of Kamiro appears in the distance.

KAMIRO — SKALA

This small village is located 51 kilometers from the city of Rhodes. Built on a small picturesque gulf, it lies across the islands of Alimia, Stroggili and Halki. There are a few inhabitants of this small fishing village which has a clean healthy climate, fresh fish and famous wine.

Swimming — water sports

The beautiful beach is ideal for swimming in the sea's clean clear water and for all types of water sports.

Fresh fish and good wine is served in the local seafood taverns of the area. There are daily excursions by caique to the islands which lie opposite the village.

KASTELLO

A medieval castle which lies in ruins but which offers a wonderful view across the sea. This Byzantine castle, which stands on a headland which projects out onto the sea, was built by the Knights in the 16th century. The coats of arms of the Grand Masters D'Amboise and Carretto can be seen on the castle walls.

KRITINIA

This village is located 5 kilometers from Kamiro-Skala and 52 kilometers from the city of Rhodes and is a typical mountain village. The inhabitants of the island, like the inhabitants of its neighbouring village Embona all came originally from Crete.

The castle of Monolitho

EMBONA

A mountainous village of Rhodes built on the slope of Mount Attabyrou at an altitude of 850m, the village has retained all of its old beauty. The houses of the village have retained not only their orginial exterior facades but their original interior design which is based on old Rhodian architecture, decoration and planning. The village is well known for its wine.

ST. ISIDORUS

This village is located 66 kilometers from Rhodes, and is yet another mountainous village which has retained the traditional life of the island. Returning once again to the main motorway the visitor reaches the village of SIANA which is located 76 kilometers from Rhodes. This village is well known for its honey. The remains of an ancient fortress lie near the village. The akrotiri of Artamitis with its panoramic view is far from the village. Unfortunately the akrotiri can only be reached on foot as there is no road suitable for cars.

MONOLITHOS

A small island which climbs up along the slope of Akromiti. The castle of Monolithos, built in the 15th century by the Knights, is not far from the village. The village is built on the cliff along the shore and offers a wonderful view. The small church of St. Pandeleimonas is located here. The sea here is ideal for swimming but the road which leads to the beach is not asphalt paved. From the village of APOLAKIA which is 92 kilometers from the city of Rhodes the main motorway leads to the abadoned Byzantine convent of "SKIADA"

KATTABIA

This village is located 107 kilometers from Rhodes and marks the end of the motorway. The church dedicated to the Virgin is one of the village's sights. If one continues on the motorway he riches the western coastline of the island passing the villages of Mesagro and Lahania. These two mountainous villages have retained the traditionally closed atmosphere of a farming village. Cars do not have access to the akrotiri of PRASONISI. A visit to the island's southern most tip can only be made on foot. Rhodes does not lack for mountainous beauty. The mountainous villages on the island are exceptionally beautiful and of course they do not offer the more established tourist conveniences and services which can be found in other areas of the island. They do, however, generously offer warm hearted island hospitality.

THE EASTERN COAST

Wonderful beaches, a clean sea and beautiful villages can be found on the eastern coast of the island. Half way along the coast stands the ancient city of Lindos.

The park **RODINI** is located 3

The beach at Haraki   *The castle «Feraklos».*

kilometers from the city and the small Muslim village of **ASGOU-ROU** is located 6 kilometers away. **KALLITHEA**, the famous seaside village, is located 10 kilometers away from the city on the main motorway. The village is built on a beautiful gulf and is surrounded by Pine and Palm trees and is well known for its hot springs which today are not used.

To the left side of the main motorway and 4 kilometers form the sea lies the lovely village of **KOSKINOU**. The village is sur-

rounded by numerous fruit orchards and other plants and has retained its old traditional Rhodian appearance. The houses are decorated with clay tiles, textiles and small courtyards lined with whitewashed cobble stones all add to the picturesquenss of this Mediterranean village. The beach covered with fine golden sand and crystal clear water is not far from the village.

Local Festivals

A festival is held on July 17 in honour of the church of St. Marina.

The beach at Tsambika

View of Phaliraki

145

Kallithea: The hot springs with drinkable mineral water

Services

There is an OTE (telephone) office. Near the village of **KALYTHIES**, 19 kilometers from the city, stands the monastery of the Prophet Amon and St. Eleousas. The popular tourist resort of **PHALIRAKI** is located 15 kilometers from the city. Phaliraki is one of the island's best and largest tourist resort. Large and small hotel complexes and fine shops next to a wonderful sandy beach and lively night Aife offers the visitor a pleasurable cosmopolitan holiday.

The beach near Kallithea

Swimming and sports

One can spend the entire day at the large beach which is one of the most beautiful on the island and which offers dressing rooms, showers, cantines and a variety of water sports such as windsurfing,.water skiing (instructions are available) or simply sunbathing.

The archaic remains at Saradapihos, the deserted castle and the monastery of the Prophet Amon and St. Eleousa are all located near this resort.

The beach at Ladiko   The beach of Lardos.

The beach at Afantou

Local Festivals

The Naval festival which lasts a week and which includes various sea competitions. The festival in honour of the monastery of the Prophet Amon and St. Eleousa is held on June 14th, on August 15 a feast is held in honour of the Virgin and on September 29th the festival in honour of St. John. In the nearby village of Kalithies a festival is held on the 14th of September in honour of the Sacred Cross and which lasts for three day.

AFANTOU

An old Rhodian village which is located 20 kilometers from the city of Rhodes, it is built not too close to the sea so that it could be protected from pirate raids in the past. Although the village is located on the road which leads to ancient Lindos, apart from the golf course, it offers no other tourists facilities although it is well known for its fruit orchards. The church dedicated to the Virgin Katholiki, which is on the road to the beach, is one of the village's sights. The church was built on the site of an older early Christian Basilica and has wall paintings which date from the 17th and 18th centuries.

Local Festivals

The Festivals which are held here are the following: On August 15th in honour of the Virgin, on October 18th in honour of St. Luke and on April 23rd in honour of St. George. All these festivals are accompanied by traditional songs and dances and local dishes which are very tasty. During the summer festivals are held with traditional popular dances. Services:There is a post office and an Ote (telephone) office in the village.

The golf course

First Aid

Medical office and a pharmacy. A turnoff of the main motorway at the village of Afantou leads to the village of Psintho which is located 32 kilometers from the city of Rhodes. This road which passes the villages of Arhipoli, Eleousa, Apollona, Platania, Dimelia, Prophet Ilias, Salako and Kalabarda rejoins the main motorway which runs along the island's western coast.

The beach at Kolymbia

KOLYMBIA

Located 25 kilometers from the capital this village has one of the most beautiful beaches and the most outstanding example of mosaic art which is found in the 6th century basilica. The beach and the church are both located on the right side of the road.

The street of Kolymbia.

EPTA PIGES

This has to be the coolest and most idylic area on the entire island. Plane trees, wells, waterfalls and a small lake create a unique natural beauty. This area offers a desirable excursion during the warm summer months. A side road which lead to the right off of the main motorway leads the Byzantine convent of Tsabika. Not to far from the main motorway an along another side road one reaches the area's beach. A beach with golden sand and crystal clear water which offers wonderful swimming and water sports. From the peak of Mount Tsabika a view stetches out at the climbers feet which is worth the climb up along the small path to the top.

ARCHAGGELOS

This large picturesque village is located 33 kilometers from the city of Rhodes. The houses are cubic shaped and the village is full of pottery workshops since the village is famed for its long tradition of pottery art. Apart from the pottery the village is also known for its fine carpets. The inhabitants, who still wear the tradition dress, have long withstood the tourist invasion

Epta Piges

and retained their traditional values and customs. The beach near the village is beautiful and not well known. A medieval castle stands above the village.

AMALONA

This village, with its wonderful beach, panoramic view and picturesque taverns and coffee houses, is located 39 kilometers from Rhodes. The medieval castle named "Pharaklos" stands on a cliff near the village. The convent of The Sacred Cross is located northwest of the village. A little past this village the road forks into two directions. The road straight ahead leads to Lindos while the road which veers to the right leads to the Bay of Bliha, one of the most magical areas on the island's eastern coast.

THE HARBOUR OF THE APOSTLE PAUL

This picturesque harbour is located below the acropolis of Lindos to the southwest. According to tradition it was at this harbour that the Apostle Paul disembarked from when he arrived on Rhodes to convert the Rhodians

Epta Piges.

158

to the religion of the Nazarene. A major festival is held each year on June 29th in honour of the church and the memory of the Apostle. At the village of KATABIA the main motorway which runs along the eastern coast joins the western coast's main motorway. Near the village of LARDOS there is a road which leads to the villages of LAERNA and ST. ISIDORUS. Road which turn off from the main motorway at the village of GENNADI lead to the villages of ASKLIPIO and BATI. At the village of Asklipio there is a church dedicated to the Virgin which was built in 1060. At Bati yet another turnoff leads to the villages of PROFYLIA and ISTRIOS. On the main motorway lies the village of LAHANIA which is located 80 kilometers from Rhodes. Another turnoff near the village of Lahania leads to the village of MESAGROS. The villages on the southern side are the most beautiful villages on the island for they have retained their pure island colour.

All these villages try to maintain the beauty of traditional life amid the natural landscape of the southern side of the island which is made up of valleys, plains and beaches.

The beach at Vliha